JN424878

NCS 기반

항공서비스 영어

BASIC AIRLINE SERVICE ENGLISH

이현옥 임영수 저

QR 코드를 찍으시면
음성화일이 지원됩니다.

양 성 원

NCS based Basic Airline Service English: NCS에 기반한 기초 항공서비스 영어

국가 직무 능력 표준(National Competency Standards- NCS)에 의거한 직업군 분류에 따르면 항공 객실 서비스를 담당하는 승무원의 직무는 객실 안전 관리, 승객 탑승 전 준비, 승객 탑승 서비스, 이륙전 서비스, 비행 중 서비스, 착륙 전 서비스, 착륙 후 서비스, 승객 하기 후 관리, 응급환자 대처, 객실 승무 관리를 하는 일입니다. 직무 정의에 다른 NCS 분류체계를 보면 다음과 같습니다.

직업군	직무	대분류	중분류	소분류	세분류
항공사 객실승부원	승무원	12. 이용 · 숙박 · 여행 · 오락 · 스포츠	03. 관광 · 레저	01. 여행 서비스	05. 항공객실 서비스

그리고, 세분류 항공객실서비스에는 총 14개의 다음과 같은 능력단위가 있습니다.

직업군	직무	능력단위(총14개)	
		능력단위코드	능력단위명(수준)
항공객실 서비스	승무원	1203010501_15v2	기내 안전관리
		1203010502_13v1	승객 탑승 전 준비
		1203010503_16v2	승객 탑승 및 이륙전 서비스
		1203010504_13v1	비행 중 서비스
		1203010505_16v2	착륙 전 서비스
		1203010506_16v2	착륙 후 서비스
		1203010507_13v1	승객 하기 후 관리
		1203010508_13v1	응급 환자 대처
		1203010509_16v2	객실 승무 관리
		1203010510_16v1	기내 음료 서비스

		1203010511_16v1	항공 서비스 업무 기본
		1203010512_16v1	항공 기내방송 업무
		1203010513_16v1	고객 만족 서비스
		1203010514_16v1	항공 서비스 매너

국가 직무 능력 표준 NCS 분류 체계에 의거하여 세분류 항공 여객 운송 서비스 중 3개의 항목을 포함하여, 세분류 항공객실서비스 14개 항목 총 17개 항목을 대략적으로 다루는 본 교재는 항공 서비스 영어 기초편으로서 항공업계 진출을 희망하는 다양한 학생들을 위해 직무 능력 표준 NCS에 의거한 세분류 항공 여객 운송 서비스 중 항공 여객 예약 관리(0904020503_16v1), 항공권 발행(0904020507_16v1), 탑승수속(0904020509_16v1)등 3개의 항공 여객 운송 서비스 전문가 항목의 내용을 일부 포함하여 실용성을 확대하였으며, 항공 객실 서비스 전문가로서 객실 서비스 규정에 따른 기내 안전 관리(1203010501_15v2), 승객 탑승 전 준비(1203010502_13v1), 승객 탑승 및 이륙전 서비스(1203010503_16v2), 비행중 서비스(1203010504_13v1), 착륙전 서비스(1203010505_16v2), 착륙후 서비스(1203010506_16v2)등 6개 항목의 영어 활용을 집중적으로 다루고 있습니다. 해당 NCS 능력단위와 코드는 다음과 같습니다.

항공 서비스 영어-기초 Airline Service English-Basic

직무명	능력단위	능력단위코드	학습모듈
기내 안전 관리 Cabin Safety Management (1203010501_15v2)	승객 탑승 전 안전 · 보안 점검하기 Safety and Security Check Before Passenger-Boarding	1203010501_15v2.1	■유/ 무
	항공기 이 · 착륙전 안전 · 보안 관리하기 Safety and Security Management Before Take-off and Landing	1203010501_15v2.2	■유/ 무

	비행 중 안전·보안 관리하기 Safaety and Security Management During the Flight	1203010501_15v2.3	■유/ 무
	착륙 후 안전·보안 점검·관리 Safaety and Security Management After Landing	1203010501_15v2.4	■유/ 무
	비상 사태 발생 시 대응하기 Responding to Emergency Situation	1203010501_15v2.5	■유/ 무
	상황별 안전안내 방송하기 Safety In-flight Announcement	1203010501_15v2.6	■유/ 무
승객 탑승 전 준비 Pre-flight Check (1203010502_13v1)	기내 서비스 용품 점검하기 In-flight Service Item	1203010502_13v1.1	■유/ 무
	서비스 설비 및 기물 점검하기 Safety Equipment	1203010502_13v1.2	■유/ 무
	특별 서비스 요청사항 Special Passenger' Request	1203010502_13v1.3	■유/ 무
승객탑승 및 이륙전 서비스 Passenger Boarding and Ground Service (1203010503_16v2)	탑승 위치 대기하기 Greet & Welcome Passengers	1203010503_16v2.1	■유/ 무
	탑승권 재확인하기 Recheck Boardig Pass	1203010503_16v2.2	■유/ 무
	좌석 안내하기 Assist Passengers' Seating	1203010503_16v2.3	■유/ 무
	수하물 정리 지원하기 Assist Passengers' Belongings	1203010503_16v2.4	■유/ 무
	특수 고객 지원하기 Special Passenger Care	1203010503_16v2.5	■유/ 무
	탑승 환영 안내방송하기 Welcome In-flight Announcement	1203010503_16v2.6	■유/ 무
비행 중 서비스 (1203010504-13v1)	기내음료 제공하기 In-flight Beverage Service	1203010504_13v1.1	■유/ 무
	기내식 제공하기 In-flight Meal Service	1203010504_13v1.2	■유/ 무
	기내 오락물 제공하기 In-flight Entertainment	1203010504_13v1.3	■유/ 무

	면세품 판매하기 In-flight Duty Free Sales	1203010504_13v1.4	■유/ 무
	객실 상태 점검하기 Cabin Check	1203010504_13v1.5	■유/ 무
착륙 전 서비스 1203010505_16v2	입국 서류 배포 및 작성 지원하기 Documentation	1203010505_16v2.1	■유/ 무
	기내용품 회수하기 Collection of In-flight Item	1203010505_16v2.2	■유/ 무
	기내 서비스 용품 및 면세품 재고 확인하기 Inventory of In-flight Service and Duty Free Item	1203010505_16v2.3	■유/ 무
	목적지 도착 안내 방송하기 Approaching In-flight Announcement	1203010505_16v2.4	■유/ 무
착륙 후 서비스 1203010506_16v2	도착 안내 방송하기 Farewell In-flight Announcement	1203010506_16v2.1	■유/ 무
	승객 하기 지원하기 Helping with Deplaning	1203010506_16v2.2	■유/ 무
	특수 고객 지원하기 Special Passenger Care	1203010506_16v2.3	■유/ 무

■ 교과개요 및 특징

본 교재는 국가 직무 능력 표준 (National Competency Standards- NCS)을 기반으로 하여, 글로벌 항공 승무원으로서 성장을 위한 기초 외국어 능력과 항공권 예약 발권 업무를 포함하여 항공기내 승객 탑승부터 착륙후 서비스까지의 영어 활용 능력을 향상 시키기 위해 편성되었습니다. 항공 서비스 영어 기초편은 NCS 분류 체계에 따른 직무명 항공 객실서비스 14개 세분류 항목을 일반적인 상황을 위주로 하여 전반적으로 다루고 있습니다. 또한, 직무 능력 표준 NCS에 의거한 세분류 항공 여객 운송 서비스 중 항공 여객 예약 관리(0904020503_16v1), 항공권 발행(0904020507_16v1), 탑승수속(0904020509_16v1)의 3항목을 일부 포함하였습니다. 그리고, 항공객실서비스 전문가로서 객실 서비스 규정에 따른 기내 안전 관리(1203010501_15v2), 승객 탑승전 준비 (1203010502_13v1), 승객 탑승 및 이륙전 서비스(1203010503_16v2), 비행중 서비스(1203010504_13v1), 착륙전 서비스(1203010505_16v2), 착륙후 서비스(1203010506_16v2)의 영어 활용을 집중적으로 다루고 있습니다. 실용적인 영어 학습을 통해, 항공권 예약· 발권, 탑승수속, 수하물 수취, 승객 탑승시 환영 인사, 탑승권 재확인, 좌석 안내, 수하물 정리, 특수 고객 지원, 탑승 환영 안내 방송하기, 기내 음료 제공하기, 기내식 제공하기, 면세품 판매하기, 객실 상태 점검하기, 입국 서류 배포 및 작성 지원하기, 기내용품 회수하기, 기내 서비스 용품 및 면세품 재고 확인하기, 목적지 도착 안내 방송하기, 도착 안내 방송하기, 승객 하기 지원하기, 특수 고객 지원하기 등의 기내 업무를 영어로 수행하는 능력을 함양할 수 있을 것입니다. 또한, 항공업계 관련 뉴스와 이슈 그리고 서비스 시점에 필요한 글로벌 에티켓과 매너에 대해 생각해 보고, 토론해 볼 수 있는 점이 조금 더 학습자들의 동기 부여와 참여를 바탕으로 한다는 점에서 커뮤니케이션에 기반한 학습이 되지 않을까 합니다. 매 학습 후에는 스스로 확인해 볼 수 있는 단어 확인과 작문 연습문제를 수록하여 탄탄한 실력을 쌓을 수 있도록 하였습니다. 완벽하지 않지만 NCS 능력 단위별 능력단위

요소를 충실히 반영하고자 한 본 교재가 항공 승무원을 꿈꾸는 학습자들에게 효과적이면서도, 실용적인 영어 학습의 동기부여가 되주길 기대합니다. 학습자 여러분께 행운이 함께하길 바랍니다.

■ 교육목표

실용적인 영어 학습을 통해, 국가 직무 능력 표준 NCS에 의거한 세분류 항공여객 운송 서비스 중 항공권 예약, 발권, 탑승수속을 일부 포함하여, 항공객실 서비스 전문가로서 객실서비스 규정에 따른 항공권 예약· 발권, 탑승수속, 수하물 수취, 승객 탑승시 환영 인사, 탑승권 재확인, 좌석 안내, 수하물 정리, 특수 고객 지원, 탑승 환영 안내 방송하기, 기내 음료 제공하기, 기내식 제공하기, 면세품 판매하기, 객실 상태 점검하기, 입국 서류 배포 및 작성 지원하기, 기내용품 회수하기, 기내 서비스 용품 및 면세품 재고 확인하기, 목적지 도착 안내 방송하기, 도착 안내 방송하기, 승객 하기 지원하기, 특수 고객 지원하기 등의 기내 업무를 영어로 수행할 수 있을 것입니다. 또한, 글로벌 항공승무원으로서 승객탑승부터 도착지 착륙후까지의 기내 상황 및 업무 전반에 걸쳐, 외국인 승객뿐 아니라, 외국인 승무원, 조종사, 현지 기내 조업 인원들과 영어로 의사소통 하여 서비스 준비 및 진행 상황에 대한 필요한 조치를 원활히 할 수 있을 것입니다.

머리말

INTRODUCTION

Based on the National Competency Standards-NCS, this textbook is designed to improve the ability of basic foreign languages for growth as a global flight attendant and the ability to communicate in English from the process of passenger boarding to after-landing services on airline service idustry, including the issuance of airline reservations. The basic English section of Airline Service covers the job name and 14 class items of Air Travel Service under the NCS classification system, with general circumstances. In addition, among class Airine Passenger Transport Service according to the job competency standard NCS, this textbook covers passenger safety management in accordance with the passenger compartment service regulations, including flight passenger booking management (0904020503_16v1), ticket issuance (09040207_16v1), boarding procedures (09040209_16v230), through practical English learning. This textbook also deals with cabin safety management (1203010501_15v2), preparation for passenger boarding (1203010502_13v1), passenger boarding and ground service (1203010503_16v2), in-flight service (1203010504_13v1), pre-landing service (1203010505_16v2), after-landing service (1203010506_16v2) following the rules of cabin service. More importantly, this textbook encourages learners to think about and discuss news and issues in regard of airline industry, global etiquette and manners required at the time of each service and learn more based on the impact of high motivation and participation of learners through communication based teaching method. After each lesson, it includes wrap up activity and writing exercise that learners can check for themselves so that they can build up their solid language skills especially productive skills focusing on speaking. We hope that this textbook, which is not perfect but faithfully reflects the capacity unit elements of NCS, will motivate learners who dream of becoming flight attendants to learn English effectively and practically. I wish you luck.

차례

CONTENTS

→PART 3
During the Flight 비행중 서비스

→PART 4
Before Landing 착륙전 서비스

→PART 5
After Landing 착륙후 서비스

PART 1

Reservation & Check-in
예약 & 탑승 수속

UNIT

1

At the Ticket Counter

예약 발권 카운터

Target Skills

1. 국가 직무 능력 표준 NCS에 의거한 세분류 항공 여객 운송 서비스 중 항공권 예약, 발권의 과정을 이해할 수 있다.
2. 국가 직무 능력 표준 NCS에 의거한 세분류 항공 여객 운송 서비스 중 항공권 예약, 발권의 과정을 영어로 수행할 수 있다.
3. 국가 직무 능력 표준 NCS에 의거한 세분류 항공 여객 운송 서비스 규정에 따라 승객의 선호 좌석을 확인하고 조치할 수 있다.

Vocabulary

1. reserve
2. flight
3. boarding pass
4. signature
5. party
6. book
7. creidt card
8. debt
9. cash
10. baggage
11. check

Target Expressions

1. May I help you?: 무엇을 도와드릴까요?
2. I'd like to reserve a ticket to NewYork.: 뉴욕행 항공권을 예약하고 싶습니다.
3. Which class would you like, sir?: 어떤 등급의 좌석을 원하십니까?
4. How many are there in your party?: 일행이 몇 분이십니까?
5. You're booked on Asiana Airlines flight 222 to New York on May 8.: 5월 8일 아시아나 항공 뉴욕행 항공권이 예약되었습니다.

Dialogue 1

Reservation

AS: Airline Staff

PAX: Passenger

AS : Asiana Airlines. **May I help you?**

PAX : **I'd like to reserve a ticket to New York.**

AS : When would you like to go, sir?

PAX : May 8.

AS : May I have your name and telephone number?

PAX : My name is Hee Jin, Kim. And my telephone number is 567-1234.

AS : **Which class would you like first, business, or economy class, sir?**

PAX : I'll take economy class.

AS : **How many are there in your party, sir?**

PAX : Two adults.

AS : Just a moment, please. Now, **you're booked on Asiana Airlines flight 222 to New York on May 8.**

PAX : Thank you.

AS : You're welcome, sir. Have a good trip.

Grammar Drill Zone

1. May I [help you / see your boarding pass / see your passport / have your signature] ?

1. May I	help you	?
	see your boarding pass	
	see your passport	
	have your signature	

2. I'd like to reserve	a ticket to New York	.
	seats for two	
	an aisle seat	

3. Which	class	would you like, sir?
	item	
	meal	

4. How many	are there in your party	?
	baggages would you like to check	

5. You're booked on	Asiana Airlines flight 222 to New York on May 8	.
	Korean Air flight 701 to Tokyo on march 21	

Practice Zone

: **Fill in the blanks to practice in pairs. Take turns to be a flight attendant and a passenger.**

Reservation

AS: Airline Staff

PAX: Passenger

AS : Asiana Airlines. (   ) I help you?

PAX : I'd like to (   ) a ticket to New York.

AS : When would you like to go, sir?

PAX : May 8.

AS : May I have your name and telephone number?

PAX : My name is Hee Jin Kim. And my telephone number is 567-1234.

AS : Which class would you like first, business, or economy class, sir?

PAX : I'll take economy class.

AS : All right, how (   ) are there in your party, sir?

PAX : Two adults.

AS : Just a moment, please. Now, you're (   ) on Asiana Airlines flight 222 to New York on May 8.

PAX : Thank you.

AS : Thank you, sir. Have a good trip.

Dialogue 2

Ticketing

AS: Airline Staff

PAX: Passenger

AS : **May I help you?**

PAX : I'd like to purchase a ticket.

AS : Did you make a reservation, sir?

PAX : Yes, I did. My reservation number is DEDNQR.

AS : All right. **May I have your name and phone number, please?**

PAX : Hee Jin Kim. My phone number is 234-5678.

AS : Thank you. It's $880.00 for round trip. **How would you like to pay, sir?**

PAX : I'll pay with my credit card. Here you are.

AS : Please wait a moment. Thank you for waiting. **May I have your signature?**

PAX : Yes.

AS : Thank you. Have a nice trip.

Grammar Drill Zone

1. May I have your [name and phone number / passport and boarding pass / signature], please?

1. May I have your	name and phone number	, please?
	passport and boarding pass	
	signature	

2. How would you like [to pay / your steak], sir?

2. How would you like	to pay	, sir?
	your steak	

Practice Zone

: Fill in the blanks to practice in pairs. Take turns to be a flight attendant and a passenger.

Ticketing

AS: Airline Staff

PAX: Passenger

AS : (   ) (   ) help you?

PAX : I'd like to purchase a ticket.

AS : Did you make a (   ), sir?

PAX : Yes, I did. My reservation number is DEDNQR.

AS : All right. (   ) (   ) have your name and phone number, please?

PAX : Hee Jin Kim. My phone number is 234-5678.

AS : Thank you. It's $880.00 for round trip. (   ) would you like to pay, sir?

PAX : I'll pay with my credit card. Here you are.

AS : Please wait a moment. Thank you for waiting. May I have your (   ) here?

PAX : Yes.

AS : Thank you. Have a nice trip.

Reading Comprehension and Discussion

: Read the passage and answer the questions. You may look up the dictionary for words.

✈ Most passengers were bound for a bank of automatic check-in machines in the centre of the hall. These **represented** an epochal shift away from the human hand and towards the robot, a transition as significant in the context of airline logistics as that from the washboard to the washing machine had once been in the domestic sphere. However,.....
(De Botton, 2010).

* epochal: 획기적인
* significant: 중대한
* logistics: 물류 업무
* washboard: 빨래판
* sphere: 영역, 구

Q1. What is the meaning of the word 'represented' in line 2?

Q2. Choose and write the opposite word of 'human hands' in this passage.

Discussion Topic

✈ Some people anticipate that most of jobs in airline industry will be replaced by machines, artificial intelligences in future. Do you agree with it and why? Please provide at least 3 reasons.

: I think most of the jobs in airline company will be still needed/replaced in future.

Because first, ____

____

Seond, ____

____

Third, ____.

Wrap Up Activity

Criss-Cross Puzzle

Down
1. arrange to have it such as a ticket for flight or a hotel room
3. a journey made by flying
4. consists of bags that you take with you when you travel
7. same as reserve:kept specially for someone on purpose
10. money can be used instantly in the form of papers or coins

Across
2. allowed to pay for goods or services later
5. written name in one's own way
6. a sum of money that you owe someone
8. group of people
9. make sure if they are in right condition

Exercise

1–5. Please translate the sentences into English.

1. 무엇을 도와드릴까요?

______________________________.

2. 일행이 몇 분이십니까?

______________________________.

3. 여기에 사인을 해 주시겠습니까?

______________________________.

4. 편도편이십니까, 왕복편이십니까?

______________________________.

5. 5월 8일 아시아나 항공 OZ 222편에 예약되셨습니다.

______________________________.

UNIT 2

Check-in

탑승 수속

Target Skills

1. 국가 직무 능력 표준 NCS에 의거한 세분류 항공 여객 운송 서비스 중 탑승수속의 과정을 이해할 수 있다.
2. 국가 직무 능력 표준 NCS에 의거한 세분류 항공 여객 운송 서비스 중 탑승수속의 과정을 영어로 수행할 수 있다.
3. 국가 직무 능력 표준 NCS에 의거한 세분류 항공 여객 운송 서비스 규정에 따라 승객의 선호 좌석을 확인하고 조치할 수 있다.
4. 항공 여객 운송 서비스 규정에 따라 승객 수하물의 종류와 갯수를 확인하고 조치할 수 있다.

Vocabulary

1. baggage claim
2. boarding gate
3. scale
4. aisle seat
5. window seat
6. describe
7. possible

Target Expressions

1. May I see your ticket and passport?: 항공권과 여권을 보여주시겠습니까?
2. Would you like an aisle seat or a window seat?: 통로 좌석을 원하십니까, 창가 좌석을 원하십니까?
3. How many baggages would you like to check?: 몇 개의 짐을 부치시겠습니까?
4. Would you put your baggage on the scale, please?: 짐을 저울에 올려주시겠습니까?
5. Do you have a baggage claim tag, sir?: 수하물표를 가지고 계십니까?
6. Would you please describe your bag?: 가방에 대해 설명해 주시겠습니까?
7. We'll let you know as soon as possible.: 최대한 빠르게 알려드리도록 하겠습니다.

Dialogue 1

Check-in

AS: Airline Staff

PAX: Passenger

AS : Good morning, sir. **May I see your ticket and passport?**

PAX : Here you are.

AS : **Would you like an aisle seat or a window seat?**

PAX : I prefer an aisle seat.

AS : All right. **How many baggages would you like to check?**

PAX : Just one.

AS : **Would you put your baggage on the scale, please?**

PAX : All right.

AS : Thank you. Here are your boarding pass and baggage claim check. Your seat is 12C and the boarding gate is 33. Boarding will begin at 5:30 pm.

PAX : Thank you.

AS : You're welcome. Have a nice trip.

Grammar Drill Zone

1. May I	see	your ticket and passport?		
	have			
	check			

2. Would you like	an aisle seat	or	a window seat	?
	business class		economy class	

3. how many	baggages	would you like to check?
	iteams	

4. would you put your baggage	on the scale	, please?
	in the overhead bin	

Practice Zone

: Fill in the blanks to practice in pairs. Take turns to be a flight attendant and a passenger.

Check-in

AS: Airline Staff

PAX: Passenger

AS : Good morning, sir. May I see your ticket and passprort?

PAX : Here you are.

AS : Would you like (   ) (   ) seat or a window seat?

PAX : I prefer an aisle seat.

AS : All right. (   ) (   ) baggages would you like to check?

PAX : Just one.

AS : Could you put your baggage on the (   ), please?

PAX : All right.

AS : Thank you. Here are your boarding pass and (   ) (   ) check. Your seat is 12C and the boarding gate is 33. Boarding will begin at 5:30 pm.

PAX : Thank you.

AS : You're welcome. Have a nice trip.

Dialogue 2

Baggage Claim

AS: Airline Staff

PAX: Passenger

AS : Good afternoon, sir. May I help you?

PAX : My baggage hasn't arrived.

AS : What's your flight number?

PAX : It's OZ 222, Asiana Airlines.

AS : **Do you have a baggage claim tag, sir?**

PAX : Yes, here you are.

AS : **Would you please describe your bag?**

PAX : Yes, It's black and there's a name tag.

AS : All right. Please wait a moment. **We'll let you know as soon as possible.**

Grammar Drill Zone

1. Do you have	a baggage claim tag the receipt	, sir?
2. Would you plase	describe explaine	your bag?
3. We'll let you know	as soon as passilde right away	.

Practice Zone

: Fill in the blanks to practice in pairs. Take turns to be a flight attendant and a passenger.

Baggage Claim

AS: Airline Staff

PAX: Passenger

AS : Good afternoon, sir. (　　　) (　　) help you?

PAX : My baggage hasn't arrived.

AS : What's your flight number?

PAX : It's OZ 222, Asiana Airlines.

AS : Do you have a baggage (　　　) tag, sir?

PAX : Yes, here you are.

AS : Would you please (　　　　) your bag?

PAX : Yes, It's black and there's a name tag.

AS : All right. Please wait a moment. We'll let you know **as soon as (　　　　).**

Reading Comprehension and Discussion

: Read the passage and answer the questions. You may look up the dictionary for words.

✈ In check in counter, passengers are supposed to put their baggages on the scale to be weighed and tagged. Then receive the baggage claim check and it should be kept well for baggage claim in destination. If your baggage is lost, the compensation for lost or damaged baggage will follow the principle of Warsaw Convention since 1929. If the Warsaw Convention is applied, it will cost $20(₩24,000) per kilogram. This means that if a 20-kilogram baggage is lost, it will give about $400(₩480,000). On the other hand, according to Montreal Protocol, it will compensate up to $1,500(₩1,800,000). Most of the developed countries follow Montreal Protocol. However, no airline is willing to pay $1,500. Passenger should prove the value of the lost baggage. When it comes to Asiana Airlines, it recieves $0.5 per baggage of $100. If you report $1,000 bag, you pay $5. If you lose this bag, you will be Compensated for $1,000 altogether. The maximum reported amount is $2,500($3,000,000).

mnews.joins.com
March 6, 2018

* destination: 목적지
* compensation: 보상
* principle: 원칙
* the Warsaw Convenfion: 바르사바 협정
* Monteal Protocol: 몬트리얼 의정서
* developed countries: 선진국들

Q1. Among the Warsaw Convention and Montreal Protocol, which one gives less amount of compensation for the lost baggage?

: ______________________________.

Q2. Among the Warsaw Convention and Montreal Protocol, which one do most developed countries follow?

: ______________________________.

Q3. According to Warsaw Convention, how much does it compensate for lost baggage of 5 kilogram?

: ______________________________.

✈ Discussion Topic (Group of 3-4)

Be an airline staff and a passenger. A Passenger Chooses one lost item. And persuade airline staff to get compensation as much as possible. Fill in the blanks with you and your group member's answers.

💻 lost item no.1 A Desk Top from Bill Gates

✉ lost item no.2 A Land Document

♉ lost item no.3 An Olympic Gold Medal

AS: Airline Staff

PAX: Passenger

AS : May I help you?

PAX : Yes. I lost my ______________________ at flight no. OZ 521 from London.

AS : Would you please describe your lost item?

PAX : It's color is ______________. And it weighs about ________kilogram. It is very valuable with three reasons as follows.

1. ____.

2. ____.

3. ____.

AS : We're terribly sorry. Let us compensate ₩______________ for your item.

Wrap Up Activity

Word Search

```
X P D Q C G D Q Y J G B K G U R G L D E
I E O E L S I A A J H M W U A A Y R T K
Z O P O S S I B L E G W O D N I W A U D
E J L C G C C T K L J R T L I Y G S D B
Q F L C G X R I Q M I B H F V H G D E R
X F U A E K R I O H K S E D N B P K X A
H T F Q R R I I B A Q K I E F P N F A Z
T X E T N S C A L E Z Q J W U C T J S M
Z S D A I G M M K F G M Q T L H J U M G
W W J E A M A W M A K G K Z J P Z I R A
O P H S B O F E N D Z Y A N C Z D D A R
C O Z P I G Z Z G D T W M K I Q F O L L
G J L I W B C L A I M B O J V K T J P B
T I J E I Z V D Z H N W W V T W T U U O
K C X V L O S I P H U C W S J R P P Q S
```

CLAIM
GATE
SCALE
AISLE
WINDOW
SEAT
DESCRIBE
POSSIBLE

Exercise

1–5. Please translate the sentences into English.

1. 항공권과 여권을 보여주시겠습니까?

____.

2. 통로 좌석을 원하십니까, 창가 좌석을 원하십니까?

____.

3. 짐을 저울에 올려주시겠습니까?

____.

4. 가방에 대해 설명해 주시겠습니까?

____.

5. 최대한 빠르게 알려드리도록 하겠습니다.

____.

PART

2

Before Take-off

이륙전 서비스

Unit 3. Safety and Security Check Before Passenger Boarding
승객 탑승 전 안전 · 보안 점검하기

Unit 4. Greet & Welcome Passengers 탑승 환영 및 좌석 안내하기

Unit 5. Assist Seating & Request 이륙전 좌석 안내와 요청사항 응대하기

Unit 6. Assist Baggage Securing 수하물 정리 지원하기

UNIT

3

Safety and Security Check Before Passenger Boarding

승객 탑승 전 안전·보안 점검하기

Target Skills

1. 객실 안전 규정에 따라 기내 안전 장비의 영어 명칭을 알 수 있다.
2. 객실 안전 규정에 따라 승객 탑승 전 기내 안전, 보안 장비를 점검하여 보고할 수 있다.
3. 객실 안전 규정에 따라 승객 탑승 전 기내 안전, 보안 장비의 위치와 사용법을 설명할 수 있다.
4. 항공 보안 및 안전 규정에 따라, 승객 탑승 전 안전, 보안에 관련 전반에 관하여 다국적 동료들 뿐 아니라 기내 조업 인원들과 의사소통 할 수 있다.

Vocabulary Zone

1. First aid equipment

   ① First aid kit 구급 상자

   ② Seal 잠금 장치

   ③ Malfunction 고장

   ④ Emergency medical kit 비상 의학상자

2. Fire extinguisher 소화기

   ① Lavatory 기내 화장실

   ② Smoke detector 연기감지장치

   ③ Circuit breaker 회로 차단기

3. Safety equipment 안전 장비
   ① Buckle 좌석벨트의 잠금장치
   ② Seatback 등받이
   ③ Fasten (벨트를) 매다
   ④ Release (벨트를) 풀다

4. Security equipment 보안 장비
   ① HW button 납치 경고 버튼

※ Survival Kit Items 비상 탈출용 생존 장비함에는 어떤 것들이 들어 있을까?

① Rations 비상식량
② Ointment eye 안약
③ Swab 살균 솜
④ Bandage strips 붕대
⑤ Light stick 야광 막대기
⑥ Signal device 불꽃조난신호장비
⑦ Triangular sling 삼각건
⑧ Sea dyemarker 해상에서 위치를 알리기 위한 물감
⑨ Signal mirror 햇빛을 이용해 조난신호를 알리는 거울
⑩ Flash light 휴대등
⑪ Megaphone 확성기
⑫ E.L.T (Emergency locator transmitter) 구조 요청을 위한 전파를 발신하는 장비

Target Expressions

1. Let me report on emergency and security equipments.: 비상 및 보안 장비에 대해 보고 드리겠습니다.
2. I'd like to report on the meals and service items.: 식사와 서비스 물품에 대해 보고 드리겠습니다.
3. It must have been used before.: 전에 사용되었던 것이 분명합니다.
4. All safety and security items are okay including smoke detector in lavatory.: 화장실 연기감지장치를 포함한 모든 안전 및 보안 장비 이상 없습니다.
5. Please press the HW button three times taking tuns from first class: 퍼스트 클래스부터 차례로 비상버튼을 세 번씩 눌러주십시오.
6. It doesn't seem to be okay.: 그것은 괜찮아 보이지 않습니다.

Dialogue 1

Pre-flight check 1

CM: Cabin Manager

FA 1: Flight Attendant 1

FA 2: Flight Attendant 2

FA 3: Flight Attendant 3

FA 1 : Dear, cabin manager, **let me report** on emergency and security equipments in first class. The emergency and security equipments are all okay in first class. The gauge of o_2 bottle indicates full. The seals of H_2 O fire extinguishers are locked firmly.

FA 2: Dear, cabin manager, **I'd like to report** on emergency and security equipments in business class. Emergency and security equipments in business class are all okay but the sealing of a fire extinguisher is broken, it **mush have been used** before.

FA 3: Dear, cabin manager, O_2 bottle in E zone of economy class is not full. Other emergency and security equipments are okay **including** smoke detector in lavatory.

CM : Thank you. Let me report them to the cabin maintenance staff and **have everything fixed**. Please report them to me again when everything has been done.

Grammar Drill Zone

1. Let me report: 보고 드리겠습니다. c.f. I'll report
2. I'd like to (동사): ( )하고자 한다. c.f. I want to
3. must have been (과거분사형): ( ) 되어졌음이 틀림없다.
4. including A: A를 포함하여

1. Let me report	on emergency and security equipments on service items in after galley	.
2. I'd like to report	on the meals and service items on the empty seats in economy class	.
3. It must have been	used before fixed by cabin mechanic	.
4. All safety and escurity items are okay including	smoke detector in lavatory fire exthinguisher in galley	.

Practice Zone

: Fill in the blanks to practice in pairs. Take turns to be a flight attendant and a passenger.

Pre-flight Check 1

CM : Cabin Manager

FA 1 : Flight Attendant 1

FA 2 : Flight Attendant 2

FA 3 : Flight Attendant 3

FA 1 : Dear, cabin manager, let me (   ) the result of checking emergency and security equipments in first class. The emergency and security equipments are all okay in first class.

FA 2 : Dear, cabin manager, emergency and security equipments in business class are all okay but the sealing of a fire extinguisher is broken, it must (   ) (   ) used before.

FA 3 : Dear, cabin manager, O_2 bottle in E zone of economy class is not full. Other emergency and security equipments including (   ) (   ) in lavatory are all okay.

CM : Thank you. Let me (   ) to the cabin maintenance staff and have everything (   ). Please report them to me again when everything has been done.

Dialogue 2

Pre-flight Check 2

CT: Captain

FA 1: Flight Attendant 1

FA 2: Flight Attendant 2

CT : Let me check secutity equipment in the cabin. Now, **please press the HW button three times taking turns from first class.**

FA 1 : Dear, captain, this is first class. Let me test HW button. (Press the HW button three times.) Thank you.

CT : Yes, it works well in first class. Thank you.

FA 2 : Dear, captain, let me test the HW button in business class. (Press the HW button three times.) Thank you.

CT : Would you press the HW button again in business class because **it doesn't seem to be okay.**

FA 2 : Captain, I am pressing it again in business class, please check it again.

CT : Yes, it works well now. Thank you.

Grammar Drill Zone

1. taking turns: 순서대로 하여
2. It seems to be ~: ~해 보인다.

1.	Please report on the service items please deplane	taking turns from first class.
2. It seems to be	broken fixed.	.

Practice Zone

: Fill in the blanks to practice in pairs. Take turns to be a flight attendant and a passenger.

Pre-flight Check 2

CT: Captain

FA 1: Flight Attendant 1

FA 2: Flight Attendant 2

CT : Let me check secutity equipment in the cabin. Now, please press the HW button three times taking (   ) from first class.

FA 1 : Dear, captain, this is first class. Let me test HW button. (Press the HW button three times.) Thank you.

CT : Yes, it works (   ) in first class. Thank you.

FA 2 : Dear, Captain, let me test the HW button in business class. (Press the HW button three times.) Thank you.

CT : Would you press the HW button again in business class because it doen't (   ) to be okay.

FA 2 : Captain, I am pressing it again in business class, please (   ) it again.

CT : Yes, it works well now. Thank you.

Reading Comprehension and Discussion

: Read the passage and answer the questions. You may look up the dictionary for words.

According to the report of CNBC, January 3, 2019 (local time), United Airlines **ban** dogs and cats from boarding for less than four month. Also, it is prohibited to fly animals for longer than eight hours in order to protect passengers or crews from being bitten or contaminated. Recently, large U.S. airlines tend to tightening restrictions on passenger flights with pets however and Korean airlines are opposed to strengthening their services in the boom of pets.

* ban: 금지하다
* prohibited: 금지된
* contaminated: 감염되다
* opposed: 반대하는

Q1. Choose and write the other word also used to mean 'ban' in this passage.

: ____.

Q2. According to the passage, why do large airlines in U.S. tend to restrict animals from boarding more than the past?

: ____

____.

Q3. Have you ever met animals in public places? What type of animal was it? How did you feel?

: ____

____

____.

✈ Discussion Topic

Should airlines in Korea allow passengers' riding with emotional support animals more or less?

> * emotional support animals: 반려동물

: I think the airlines in Korea should allow/not allow passengers riding with emotional support animals more.

Because ____

____

____

____

____

____.

Wrap Up Activity

Unscramble the letters and write the words in right order.

1. ceeergmny ______________
2. oayatrlv ______________
3. tkaeabcs ______________
4. agueg ______________
5. eukclb ______________
6. ntasfe ______________
7. eselaer ______________
8. xriguethnise ______________
9. meqtuipen ______________
10. certsuiy ______________

Exercise

1–5. Please translate the sentences into English.

1. 매니저님, 비상 장비 및 보안 장비 점검 보고 드리겠습니다.

______________________________.

2. 퍼스트 클래스의 비상 장비 및 보안 장비는 이상 없습니다.

______________________________.

3. 매니저님, 비즈니스 클래스의 소화기의 잠금장치가 깨져 있습니다.

______________________________.

4. 이코노미 클래스에 있는 E 구역의 산소호흡기의 산소가 가득 차 있지 않습니다.

______________________________.

5. 화장실 연기 감지기를 포함하여 다른 비상 장비 및 보안 장미는 모두 이상 없습니다.

______________________________.

UNIT

4

Greet & Welcome Passengers

탑승 환영 및 좌석 안내하기

Target Skills

1. 객실 서비스 규정에 따라 항공기 이착륙 전 객실 서비스 규정에 따라, 승객의 항공기 탑승 전 각자에게 부여된 임무를 수행하기 위하여 해당 근무 지역에서 탑승을 위해 대기할 수 있다.
2. 객실 서비스 규정에 따라 승객 탑승 시 객실 서비스 규정에 따라, 바른 자세와 밝은 표정으로 환영 인사를 할 수 있다.
3. 객실 서비스 규정에 따라 탑승 승객에 따른 눈높이 자세를 취하며 대화를 이어갈 수 있다.
4. 객실 서비스 규정에 따라 승객의 출발 일시와 목적지를 확인할 수 있다.

Vocabulary Zone

① aboard

② boarding pass

③ aisle

④ front

⑤ middle

⑥ back

⑦ cabin

⑧ flight

Target Expressions

1. Welcome aboard.: 탑승을 환영합니다.
2. May I see your boarding pass, please?: 탑승권을 보여주시겠습니까?
3. Please take this aisle.: 이쪽 통로를 이용하시겠습니까?
4. It's in the back/front/middle/the other side of the cabin.: 기내 뒷쪽/앞쪽/가운데쪽/건너편쪽입니다.
5. You're welcome.: 천만에요.
6. Enjoy your flight, sir/ma'am.: 즐거운 비행 되십시오.
7. May I help you?: 무엇을 도와드릴까요?
8. Your seat number is 45K.: 손님 좌석은 45K입니다.
9. Please come this way.: 이쪽으로 오십시오.
10. It's a window/an aisle seat.: 창가/통로쪽 자리입니다.
11. Your seat is right here: 손님 좌석은 바로 여기입니다.

Dialogue 1

At Boarding Position

FA: Flight Attendant

PAX: Passenger

FA : Good morning, **Welcome aboard. May I see your boarding pass, please?**

PAX: Yes, here it is.

FA : Thank you. It's 35A. **Please take this aisle. It's in the back of the cabin.**

PAX: Thank you.

FA : You're welcome. **Enjoy your flight, sir/ma'am.**

Grammar Drill Zone

1. Welcome aboard.: 탑승을 환영합니다.
2. May I see your boarding pass, please?: 탑승권을 보여주시겠습니까?
3. Please take this aisle.: 이쪽 통로를 이용하시겠습니까?
4. It's in the back/front/middle/the other side of the cabin.: 기내 뒷쪽/앞쪽/가운데쪽/건너편쪽입니다.
5. You're welcome.: 천만에요.
6. Enjoy your flight, sir/ma'am.: 즐거운 비행 되십시오.

1. Welcome	aboard to Korea	.
2. May I see your	boarding pass ticket	please?
3. Please take	this that	aisle.
4. It's in the	back front middle	of the cabin.

5. You're welcome / so kind to say so .

6. Enjoy your / Have a nice flight, sir.

Practice Zone

: Fill in the blanks to practice in pairs. Take turns to be a flight attendant and a passenger.

At Boarding Position

FA: Flight Attendant

PAX: Passenger

FA : Good morning, Welcome (   ). (   ) (   ) see your boarding pass, please?

PAX : Yes, here it is.

FA : Thank you. Your seat is 55A. Please (   ) this aisle. It's in the back of the cabin on your right.

PAX : Thank you.

FA : You're (   ). (   ) your flight, sir/ma'am.

Dialogue 2

At Duty Zone

FA: Flight Attendant

PAX: Passenger

FA : Welcome aboard. May I help you, sir/ma'am?

PAX : I'm looking for my seat.

FA : May I see your boarding pass, please?

PAX : Here it is.

FA : Thank you. Your seat number is 45K. Please come this way.
(FA guides PA to the seat.)

FA : **Your seat is right here. It's an aisle seat.**

PAX : Thank you.

FA : You're welcome. Please enjoy your flight.

Grammar Drill Zone

1. May I help you?: 무엇을 도와드릴까요?
2. Your seat number is 45K.: 손님 좌석은 45K입니다.
3. Please come this way.: 이쪽으로 오십시오.
4. It's a window/an aisle seat.: 창가/통로쪽 자리입니다.

1.	May	I help you?
	How can	

2.	Your seat number	is 45K.
	Your seat	
	It	

3. Please	come this	way.
	go that	

4. It's	an aisle	seat.
	a window	

Practice Zone

: Fill in the blanks to practice in pairs. Take turns to be a flight attendant and a passenger.

At Duty Zone

FA: Flight Attendant

PAX: Passenger

FA : ( ) aboard. May I ( ) you, sir/máam?

PAX : I'm looking for my seat.

FA : May I see your boarding ( ), please?

PAX : Here it is.

FA : Thank you. Your seat number is 45K. Please ( ) this way.

(FA guides PA to the seat)

FA : Your seat is ( ) here. It's an aisle seat.

PAX : Thank you.

FA : You're ( ). Please ( ) your flight.

Reading Comprehension and Discussion

: Read the passage and answer the questions. You may look up the dictionary for words.

In Korea, it's regarded to be polite to greet with a bow when you welcome customers. However in most western countries, one's head is supposed to be straight to have sincere eye-contact with bright smile. When the passenger-boarding starts, approximately 20-30 minutes in advance of departure time, cabin crews stand by the given position depending on their duties assigned by a cabin manager of the flight. It is important moment not only to provide good first impression of the airline company and their quality of service but also to build a positive **rapport** with passengers of their own zones.

* polite: 예의바른
* approximately: 대략
* first impression: 첫인상
* quality: 양질의, 품질

Q1. The word 'rapport' in this passage means ______________________.

Q2. What's the difference between Koreans and Westerns in welcoming customers?

: ______________________.

Q3. Have you ever worked in service industry? How did you welcome customers?

______________________.

✈ Discussion Topic

Share your experience with foreigners especially about the way to get closed.

: When I was in Vietnam last year, I could make friends with foreigners by.......

____

____

____

____

____

______________________.

Wrap Up Activity

〈Check what you have to do during boarding〉-pair work

- ☐ Greet with eye-contact.
- ☐ Speak in English to greet a passenger looks like Korean.
- ☐ Stand by the galley.
- ☐ Allow passengers to change their seats on their own.
- ☐ Ask a mother if her child needs a give-away item during the flight.
- ☐ Welcome every passenger with bright smile.
- ☐ Stand by to lift passenger's heavy baggage alone.
- ☐ Bring a cup of warm water for a thirsty child.
- ☐ Say instantly to the passenger that we have no more newspapers left.
- ☐ Make a duty-free sales announcement.
- ☐ Check the lavatory if it is cleaned.
- ☐ Provide hot coffee right before take-off.

Exercise

1–5. Please translate the sentences into English.

1. 탑승을 환영합니다.

____.

2. 탑승권을 보여주시겠습니까?

____.

3. 이쪽 통로를 이용해 주십시오.

____.

4. 손님의 좌석은 기내 반대편에 있습니다.

____.

5. 곧 가져다 드리겠습니다.

____.

UNIT

5

Assist Seating & Request

이륙전 좌석 안내와 요청사항 응대하기

Target Skills

1. 객실 서비스 규정에 따라, 탑승중 승객의 요청에 신속히 응대할 수 있다.
2. 객실 서비스 규정에 따라, 탑승 승객에 따른 눈높이 자세를 취하며 대화를 이어갈 수 있다.
3. 객실 서비스 규정에 따라, 승객에게 좌석 설비 사용법을 안내할 수 있다.
4. 객실 서비스 규정에 따라, 좌석 상태를 파악하여, 조치할 수 있다.

Vocabulary

1. 단위 명사

① a glass of water

② a cup of juice

③ a cup of coffee

④ a piece paper

⑤ a spoonful of sugar

2. 곧, 신속하게

① right away

② as soon as possible

③ immediately

3. cooperation
4. arrangement
5. inconvenience

Target Expressions

1. May I have a glass of water?: 물 한잔 주시겠습니까?
2. Let me get it for you, right away.: 금방 가져다 드리겠습니다.
3. Let me check if there's what I can do.: 제가 도와드릴 수 있는지 알아보겠습니다.
4. Thank you for waiting.: 기다려 주셔서 감사합니다.
5. Please come with me.: 저를 따라 와주십시오.
6. Thank you for your cooperation: 협조해 주셔서 감사합니다.
7. There has been a mistake in seat arrangement.: 좌석 배정에 문제가 있었나 봅니다.
8. I'm terribly sorry for the inconvenience.: 불편을 드려 대단히 죄송합니다.
9. If you need anything during the flight, please let us know.: 비행중 필요한 것이 있으시면 알려주십시오.

Dialogue 1

Passenger Request–Drink

FA: Flight Attendant

PAX: Passenger

PAX : Excuse me, **may I have a glass of water?**

FA : Certainly. **Let me get it for you, right away.**

PAX : Here's your water, sir/ma'am.

PA : Thank you.

PAX : You're welcome. Enjoy your flight.

Grammar Drill Zone

1. May I have ~: ~주실 수 있나요?
2. Let me get it for you.: 가져다 드리겠습니다.

1. May I have	a glass of water	?
	a cup of coffee	
	a piece of paper	
	a pound of sugar	

2. Let me get it for you,	right away	.
	immediately	
	as soon as possible	

Practice Zone

: Fill in the blanks to practice in pairs. Take turns to be a flight attendant and a passenger.

Passenger Request–Drink

FA: Flight Attendant

PAX: Passenger

PAX : Excuse me, ( ) ( ) **have** a glass of water?

FA : Certainly. ( ) ( ) **get it for you**, right away.

PAX : Here's your water, sir/ma'am.

PA : Thank you.

PAX : You're welcome. Enjoy your flight.

Dialogue 2

Passenger Request-Seperated Seats

FA: Flight Attendant

PAX: Passenger

PAX : Excuse me. I am seperated from my friend over there, and I would like to seat with her. Is it possible?

FA : **Let me check if there's what I can do.** Please wait a moment.

(After a while)

FA : **Thank you for waiting, sir.** We have some empty seats in the back of the cabin. Would you like to seat together in the back?

PAX : Yes, I would. Thank you.

FA : My pleasure. **Please come with me.**
Here they are. Enjoy your flight.

Grammar Drill Zone

1. Let me check if there's what I can do.: 제가 도와드릴 수 있는지 알아보겠습니다.
2. Thank you for waiting.: 기다려 주셔서 감사합니다.
3. Please come with me.: 저를 따라 와주십시오.

1. Let me check if	there's what I can do	.
	it can be arranged	
2. Thank you for	waiting	.
	patience	
3. Please come	with me	.
	this way	

Passenger Request–Seperated Seats

FA: Flight Attendant

PAX: Passenger

PAX : Excuse me. I am seperated from my friend over there, and I would like to seat with her. Is it possible?

FA : ( ) ( ) ( ) if there's what I can do. Please wait a moment.

(After a while)

FA : ( ) ( ) ( ) waiting, sir. We have some empty seats in the back of the cabin. Would you like to seat together in the back?

PAX : Yes, I would. Thank you.

FA : My pleasure. Please ( ) with me.
Here they are. Enjoy your flight.

Dialogue 3

Passenger Request–Double Seat

FA: Flight Attendant

PAX 1: Passenger 1

PAX 2: Passenger 2

PAX 1 : Excuse me. There is someone in my seat.

FA : What's your seat number, sir? May I see your boarding pass?

PAX 1 : Here you are. It's 24D.

(FA goes to 24D with PAX 1-the passenger first asked.)

(FA asks to PAX 2-the passenger occupying 24D.)

FA : Excuse me to bother you, sir. May I see your boarding pass?

PAX 2 : All right, here it is.

FA : Your seat number is 24D. too. **Thank you for your cooperation.**

(FA sincerely apologizes to PAX 1.)

FA : I'm terribly sorry sir. **There has been a mistake in seat arrangement.** Let me get you a new seat number right away. Please wait a moment.

PAX 1 : Sure.
(After reporting it to the ground staff)

FA : Thank you for waiting, sir. Your seat has been assigned to 17G. Please come this way. Here it is. May I get you something to drink?

PAX 1 : No, thanks.

FA : **I'm terribly sorry for the inconvenience. If you need anything during the flight, please let us know.** Please enjoy your flight.

Grammar Drill Zone

1. Thank you for your cooperation: 협조해 주셔서 감사합니다.
2. There has been a mistake in seat arrangement.: 좌석 배정에 문제가 있었나 봅니다.
3. I'm terribly sorry for the inconvenience.: 불편을 드려 대단히 죄송합니다.
4. If you need anything during the flight, please let us know.: 비행중 필요한 것이 있으시면 알려주십시오.

1. Thank you for your	cooperation attention	.
2. There has been a mistake in	seat arrangement baggage securing delivering	.
3. I'm terribly sorry	for the inconvenience to have kept you waiting	.
4. If you need anything	during the flight ofter take-off	, please let us know.

Passenger Request-Double Seat

FA: Flight Attendant

PAX 1: Passenger 1

PAX 2: Passenger 2

PAX 1 : (   ) me, there is someone in my seat.

FA : What's your seat number, sir? May I see your (   ) (   )?

PAX 1 : Here you are. It's 24D.
(FA Goes to 24D with PAX 1-the passenger first asked.)
(FA asks to PAX 2-the passenger occupying 24D.)

FA : Excuse me to (   ) you, sir. May I see your boarding pass?

PAX 2 : All right, here it is.

FA : Your seat number is 24D. too. Thank you for your (   ).
(FA sincerely apologizes to PAX 1.)

FA : I'm terribly sorry sir. There has been a mistake in ( ) ( ). Let me get you a new seat number right away. Please wait a moment.

PAX 1 : Sure.
(After reporting it to the ground staff)

FA : Thank you for waiting, sir. Your seat has been assigned to 17G. Please come this way. Here it is. ( ) ( ) get you something to drink?

PAX 1 : No, thanks.

FA : I'm ( ) ( ) for the inconvenience. If you need anything during the flight, please let us ( ). Please enjoy your flight.

Reading Comprehension and Discussion

: Read the passage and answer the questions. You may look up the dictionary for words.

Airline cabin crews must have some knowledge of the aircraft. Most passengers expect the cabin crew to know a lot more than we think, and ask various questions to the crew member. For example, flight theory, like the principle that an aircraft can fly. This flight theory has been recently asked as an interview question at an airline cabin crew recruitment interview.

So, what is the principle of the four forces to fly an aircraft? It is 'thrust', 'drag', 'lift', 'gravity'.

The thrust is that the engine pushes the air to the back of the aircraft and causes the aircraft to move forward through the action-reaction.

Drag is a kind of the force, caused by air acting against the aircraft and acting behind the aircraft. Without air there would be no drag.

The lift is the force made by the difference of the pressure between the top and bottom of the wing.

Finally, gravity is the weight of the aircraft and the earth pulling together.

If so, what would happen to an aircraft if gravity was greater than lift?

* knowledge: 지식	* aircraft: 항공기
* various: 다양한	* theory: 이론
* recruitement: 채용	* force: 힘
* thrust: 추진력	* drage: 항력
* lift: 양력	* gravity: 중력

Q1. Why do cabin crews must have some background knowledge about an aircraft theory?

: ______________________________

______________________________.

Q2. According to the passage, the weight of the aircraft is closely related to ______________ among all four forces of thrust, drag, lift and gravity.

Q3. What do you think will happen to an aircraft if gravity is greater than lift?

: ______________________________

______________________________.

✈ Discussion Topic

What will you do, if a passenger asks you something you do not know? And share your experience that a customer asked you about something you did't know.

If a passenger asks me about somsthing I don't know, I will____________

____because

____

____

____.

When I worked at ____________________, One customer asked me,

"____?"

So, I answered,

"____

____."

Wrap Up Activity

Fill in the blanks with appropriate answers given below.

PAX: Passenger

FA: Flight Attendant

1. PAX: Excuse me. There is someone in my seat.

   FA: ______________________________.

2. PAX: May I have a cup of coffee?

   FA: ______________________________.

3. PAX: I am seperated from my friend over there.

   FA: ______________________________.

4. PAX: Thank you.

FA: ______________________.

5. PAX: No. thanks.

FA: ____.

1. It's my pleasure.
2. May I see your boarding pass?
3. Let me check if I can help you.
4. If you need anything during the flight, please let us know.
5. Certainly. Let me get it for you.

Exercise

1–5. Please translate the sentences into English.

1. 곧 가져다 드리겠습니다.

____.

2. 불편을 드려 대단히 죄송합니다.

____.

3. 제가 도와드릴 수 있는지 알아보겠습니다.

____.

4. 좌석 배정에 문제가 있었나 봅니다.

____.

5. 비행중 필요한 것이 있으시면, 저희에게 알려주십시오.

____.

UNIT

6

Assist Baggage Securing

수하물 정리 지원하기

Target Skills

1. 객실 서비스 규정에 따라, 탑승중 승객의 수하물의 기내반입 가능여부를 판단하여 안내할 수 있다.
2. 객실 서비스 규정에 따라, 수하물의 종류에 따른 보관 위치를 안내할 수 있다.
3. 항공기 안전 규정에 따라, 이륙전 유동 수하물 고정하여 안전한 이륙준비를 할 수 있다.
4. 항공기 안전 규정에 따라, 수하물의 종류에 따른 적절한 보관 위치를 안내하여 조치할 수 있다.

Vocabulary Zone

1. closet
2. overhead bin
3. galley
4. take off
5. landing
6. stow
7. put
8. electronic device
9. heavy
10. turn off

Target Expressions

1. Is this bag yours?: 이 가방은 당신 것입니까?
2. I'm afraid all the aisles should be cleaned during take off and landing.: 이착륙 동안에는 모든 기내 통로가 치워져 있어야 합니다.
3. Please put your bag in the overhead bin.: 가방은 머리위 보관함에 넣어 주십시오.
4. This bag is too heavy to keep in the overhead bin.: 이 가방은 너무 커서 머리위 보관함에 보관할 수 없습니다.
5. Would you keep your bag under the seat in front of you?: 손님의 가방은 앞좌석 아래에 보관해 주시겠습니까?
6. May I keep it in the closet?: 그 짐을 옷장에 보관해 드려도 되겠습니까?
7. Please wait in your seat.: 좌석에서 기다려 주십시오.

Dialogue 1

Baggage in the Aisle

FA: Flight Attendant

PAX: Passenger

FA : Excuse me, sir. **Is this bag yours?**

PAX : Yes, it's mine.

FA : **I'm afraid all the aisles should be cleaned during take off and landing. Please put your bag in the overhead bin.**

PAX : All right, but there's no space in the overhead bin.

FA : Let me help you, sir.

(FA makes space in the overhead bin by pushing other bags a little to each other.)

FA : Please put your bag here, sir.

PAX : All right. Thank you.

FA : It's my pleasure.

Grammar Drill Zone

1. Is this bag yours?: 이 가방은 당신 것입니까?
2. I'm afraid all the aisles should be cleaned during take off and landing.: 이착륙 동안에는 모든 기내 통로가 치워져 있어야 합니다.
3. Please put your bag in the overhead bin.: 가방은 머리위 보관함에 넣어 주십시오.

1. Is this	bag stroller	yours?
2. I'm afraid	all the aisles should be cleaned electronic devices should be turned off	during take-off and landing.
3. Please put your bag	in the overhead bin under your seat	.

Baggage in the Aisle

FA: Flight Attendant

PAX: Passenger

FA : Excuse me, sir. Is this bag (   )?

PAX : Yes, it's mine.

FA : I'm (   ) all the aisles should be cleaned (   ) take off and landing. Please put your bag in the overhead bin.

PAX : All right, but there's no space in the overhead bin.

FA : Let me help you, sir.
(FA makes space in the overhead bin by pushing other bags a little to each other.)

FA : Please (   ) your bag here, sir.

PAX : All right. Thank you.

FA : It's my (   ).

Dialogue 2

Heavy Baggage

FA: Flight Attendant

PAX: Passenger

FA : Excuse me, sir. **This bag is too heavy to stow in the overhead bin. Would you keep it under the seat in front of you?**

PAX : All right.

FA : Thank you. Enjoy your flight.

Grammar Drill Zone

1. This bag is too heavy to keep in the overhead bin.: 이 가방은 너무 커서 머리 위 보관함에 보관할 수 없습니다.

2. Would you keep your bag under the seat in front of you?: 손님의 가방은 앞좌석 아래에 보관해 주시겠습니까?

1. This bag is too	heavy	to keep	in the overhead bin	.
	big		cabin	

2. Would you keep it	under the seat in front of you	?
	in the overhead bin	

Practice Zone

: Fill in the blanks to practice in pairs. Take turns to be a flight attendant and a passenger.

Heavy Baggage

FA: Flight Attendant

PAX: Passenger

FA : Excuse me, sir. This bag is (   ) heavy (   ) stow in the overhead bin. Would you keep it under the (   ) in front of you?

PAX : All right.

FA : Thank you. Enjoy your (   ).

Dialogue 3

Oversize Baggage

FA: Flight Attendant

PAX: Passenger

FA : Sir, your bag is too big to keep in the overhead bin or under the seat. **May I keep it in the closet?**

PAX : Yes, please.

FA : Let me get it for you after landing. **Please wait in your seat when you deplane.**

PAX : Thank you.

FA : It's my pleasure. Have a nice flight.

Grammar Drill Zone

1. May I keep it in the closet?: 그 짐을 옷장에 보관해 드려도 되겠습니까?
2. Please wait in your seat when you deplane.: 내리실 때 좌석에서 기다려 주십시오.

1. May I keep it	in the closet	?
	the overhead bin	
	the galley	

2. Please wait	in your seat	.
	in front of the cabin	

Practice Zone

: Fill in the blanks to practice in pairs. Take turns to be a flight attendant and a passenger.

Oversize Baggage

FA: Flight Attendant

PAX: Passenger

FA : Sir, your bag is too big to keep in the (   ) (   ) or under the (   ). May I keep it in the closet?

PAX : Yes, please.

FA : Let me get it for you after (   ). Please (   ) in your seat when you deplane.

PAX : Thank you.

FA : It's my pleasure. Have a nice flight.

Reading Comprehension and Discussion

: Read the passage and answer the questions. You may look up the dictionary for words.

It is said that the job position of cabin crew member is the flower of all service industry. Providing good service based on safety is regarded to be the cabin crew's main duty as most of people can think of. But what is a good service? A good service simply doesn't come easily. It is the fruit of the efforts of all employees of the airline. All crew members must collaborate during the long flight hours, one crew member's doing well is not enough to create customer satisfaction and provide excellent service. Achieveing an efficient service design in contact with customers is ultimately up to the team work of all crew members. It is also the role of the crew members to determine the overall image of the airline and make it an important part of marketing.

- ✱ employee: 직원
- ✱ collaborate: 협업하다
- ✱ satisfaction: 만족
- ✱ ultimately: 궁극적으로, 결국
- ✱ determine: 결정짓다

Q1. According to the passage, how can a good service be achieved?

:____

____.

Q2. What are the roles of cabin crews?

:____

____.

✈ Discussion Topic

What do you think is the most important aptitude(quality) of good flight attendant?

:The most important aptitude as a cabin crew is ___________because______

____

____

____

____.

Wrap Up Activity

Fill in the blanck with appropriate words.

A. Please turn off all electronic devices during take off and __________.

B. Please put your bag in the ___________ bin.

C. ______________ is to make a decision.

D. _________ is in-flight kitchen that cre members prepare service.

E. ______________ means helping each other for better performance.

F. Airline service goes on after __________ , too.

G. Fire extinguisher is an emergency equipment to _____ out the fire.

H. May I keep your bag in the ___________?

• galley	• determine
• cooperation	• deplaning
• put	• closet
• overhead	• landing

Exercise

1–5. Please translate the sentences into English.

1. 이 가방은 당신 것입니까?

______________________________.

2. 이착륙 동안에는 모든 기내 통로가 치워져 있어야 합니다.

______________________________.

3. 이 가방은 좌석 아래에 넣어 주십시오.

______________________________.

4. 그 짐을 옷장에 보관해 드려도 되겠습니까?

______________________________.

5. 이 가방은 너무 무거워 머리위 보관함에 두실 수 없습니다.

______________________________.

PART 3

During the Flight

비행중 서비스

UNIT

7

Safety and Security Management During the Flight

비행중 항공기 안전·보안 관리하기

Target Skills

1. 항공기 안전 규정에 따라 항공기 이착륙전, 비행중 안전사항을 안내하고 점검할 수 있다.
2. 객실 안전 규정에 따라 승객에게 좌석 벨트 착용 안내를 정확하게 할 수 있다.
3. 객실 안전 규정에 따라 비상구 위치에 착석한 승객에게 비상시 행동 요령과 업무 협조를 안내할 수 있다.
4. 객실 안전 규정에 따라 미착석 승객을 확인하고 착석을 유도할 수 있다.
5. 객실 안전 규정에 따라 창문 덮개, 좌석앞 선반, 등받이를 원위치할 수 있도록 안내할 수 있다.

Vocabulary Zone

1. emergency
2. evacuate
3. upright
4. prepare
5. expect
6. turbulence
7. securely
8. deplane
9. moderate
10. severe

Target Expressions

1. This is an emergency exit door for emergency.: 이 좌석은 비상시만을 위한 비상구입니다.
2. Passengers in emergency exit seats are supposed to help flight atendants to evacuate passengers in emergency.: 비상구 좌석에 앉아계신 승객들께서는 비상시 승무원을 도와 승객들의 탈출을 도우셔야 합니다.
3. We are preparing for take-off.: 이륙준비를 하고 있습니다.
4. Please fasten your seatbelt.: 좌석벨트를 매주시기 바랍니다.
5. Return your seat back to the upright position, please.: 좌석 등받이를 제 자리로 해 주 시기 바랍니다.
6. Please press the button on your right.: 오른쪽에 있는 버튼을 눌러 주십시오.
7. We are expecting some turbulence.: 불안정한 기류관계로 기체가 약간 흔들릴 것으로 예상됩니다.
8. Please also check if the seat belt of your child is securely fastened.: 자녀의 좌석 벨트가 잘 매어져 있는지 또한 확인해 주십시오.

Dialogue 1

Passengers in Emergency Exit Seats

FA: Flight Attendant

PAX: Passenger

FA : **This is an emergency exit door only for emergency. Passengers in emergency exit seats are supposed to help flight atendants to evacuate passengers in emergency.** Please exit first and help other passengers with deplaning. Do you agree?

PAX : Yes, I will.

FA : Please read this emergency exit seat guide.

PAX : All right.

FA : Thank you for your cooperation.

Grammar Drill Zone

1. This is an emergency exit door for emergency.: 이 좌석은 비상시만을 위한 비상구입니다.
2. Passengers in emergency exit seats are supposed to help flight atendants to evacuate passengers in emergency.: 비상구 좌석에 앉아계신 승객들께서는 비상시 승무원을 도와 승객들의 탈출을 도우셔야 합니다.

1. This is an emergency exit	door only for emergency	.
	way	
	light	

2. Passengers in emergency exit seats are supposed to	help flight atendants to evacuate passengers in emergency	.
	exit first to help other passengers with deplaning	

Practice Zone

: Fill in the blanks to practice in pairs. Take turns to be a flight attendant and a passenger.

Passengers in Emergency Exit Seats

FA: Flight Attendant

PAX: Passenger

FA : This is an (   ) exit door only for emergency. Passengers in emergency exit seats are supposed to (   ) flight attendants to (   ) passengers in emergency. Please exit first and help other passengers with deplaning. Do you agree?

PAX : Yes, I will.

FA : Please read this emergency exit seat guide.

PAX : All right.

FA : Thank you for your (   ).

Dialogue 2

Safety Check before Take-off

FA: Flight Attendant

PAX: Passenger

FA : Excuse me. **We are preparing for take-off. Please fasten your seat belt. And return your seat back to the upright position, please.**

PAX: Sure, but I don't know how to return this seat back.

FA : Let me help you. **please press the button on your right.**

PAX: Thank you.

FA : It's my pleasure. Enjoy your flight.

Grammar Drill Zone

1. We are preparing for take-off.: 이륙준비를 하고 있습니다.
2. Please fasten your seatbelt.: 좌석벨트를 매주시기 바랍니다.
3. Return your seat back to the upright position, please.: 좌석 등받이를 제 자리로 해 주 시기 바랍니다.

1. We are preparing for [take-off / landing].

2. Please [fasten your seat belt / buckle up].

3. Return your [seat back / tray table] to the upright position, please.

Practice Zone

: Fill in the blanks to practice in pairs. Take turns to be a flight attendant and a passenger.

Safety Check before Take-off

FA: Flight Attendant

PAX: Passenger

FA : Excuse me. We are ( ) for take-off. Please ( ) your seat belt. And ( ) your seat back to the upright position, please.

PAX : Sure, but I don't know how to return this seat back.

FA : Let me help you. please press the ( ) on your right.

PAX : Thank you.

FA : It's my pleasure. Enjoy your flight.

Dialogue 3

Expecting Turbulence

FA: Flight Attendant

PAX: Passenger

FA : Excuse me. **We are expecting some turbulence.** Please fasten your seatbelt. Return your seat back and tray table to the upright position.

PAX : All right.

FA : **Please also check if the seatbelt of your child is securely fastened.**

PAX : Sure.

FA : Please return your bag to the overhead bin.

PAX : Yes. I will.

FA : Thank you, sir.

Grammar Drill Zone

1. We are expecting some turbulence.: 불안정한 기류관계로 기체가 약간 흔들릴 것으로 예상됩니다.
2. Please also check if the seatbelt of your child is securely fastened.: 자녀의 좌석 벨트가 잘 매어져 있는지 또한 확인해 주십시오.

1. We are expecting	some	turbulence.
	moderate	
	severe	

2. Please also check if	the seatbelt	of your child	is securely fastened	.
	the tray table		in the upright position	
	seat back		in the upright position	

Practice Zone

: Fill in the blanks to practice in pairs. Take turns to be a flight attendant and a passenger.

Expecting Turbulence

FA: Flight Attendant

PAX: Passenger

FA : Excuse me. We are expecting some ( ). Please fasten your ( ) ( ). Return your seat( ) and tray table to the upright position.

PAX : All right.

FA : Please also check if the seatbelt of your child is securely ( ).

PAX : Sure.

FA : Please ( ) your bag to the overhead bin.

PAX : Yes. I will.

FA : Thank you, sir.

Reading Comprehension

: Read the passage and answer the questions. You may look up the dictionary for words.

There are frequent arguments between airlines and passengers these days. Not long ago, there was a row between a flight attendant and a disabled passenger.

A 31-year-old man from San Francisco in the U.S. was refused to sit in an emergency exit seat for wearing a prosthetic leg on an airplane heading for Seoul from Beijing, China. The flight attendant asked the man sitting in an emergency exit seat to be moved to other seat however, the man said he had the ability to help escape passengers under safety regulations. The male passenger claimed that he had been using his prosthetic leg since he was 11 years old. And that he had been using emergency exit seat several times till then because he had no problem with his behavior as he enjoyed a skateboard. However, he ultimately had to move his seat.

U.S. media reports that the Federal Aviation Administration's guideline says seat restrictions depend on mental problems, not physical defects such as prosthetics. However, the airline says it was for passenger safety and that the final decision on the emergency exit assignment is for the airline.

* argument: 논쟁
* row: 심각한 의견 대립
* disabled: 장애를 가진
* prosthetic: 인공기관의(보철의)
* Federal Aviation Administration: 미국 연방 항공국
* restriction: 규제
* mental: 정신적인
* physical: 신체적인
* assignment: 배정

Q1. According to the passage, where did the argument happen?

:In ____________, ________________

Q2. What was the reason for the flight attendant to have the male passenger moved to the other seat?

:The reason was because the male passenger.....

____.

Q3. What were the reasons for the male passenger claiming to sit on emergency exit seat?

:____

____

____.

✈ Discussion Topic

"Do airlines have to regulate passengers with prosthetics sitting in emergency exit seats?"

1. Write the guideline of Federal Aviation Administration and the regulation of the airline company.

Opinion	Federal Aviation Administration	Airline company
"Can passengers with prosthetics sit in emergency exit seats?"	Yes, because..... ______ ______ ______ ______ ______ ______.	No, because..... ______ ______ ______ ______ ______ ______.

2. Which idea do you support?

: ______

3. Disscuss to choose the opinion of your team.

:We support the opinion of ______ because......

______

______.

Wrap Up Activity

Use the words in the box to complete the sentences.

1. I would like to ________________ later because it takes time for me to prepare my wheelchair.

2. There are 6 exit doors in this aircraft and they are only for the ____________.

3. Please help other passengers ________________. Do you agree?

4. I ___________ them to be all right during the rest of the flight time.

5. Ladies and gentlemen, if the seat belt sign blinks twice we might meet ___________ turbulence.

6. Please check to see if your seat belt is _____________ fastened.

7. When your seat back and tray table are ________ position then you are ready to land.

8. To ________ for departure, please turn off all electronic devices.

• deplane	• emergency
• evacuate	• expect
• moderate	• prepare
• securely	• upright

Exercise

1–5. Please translate the sentences into English.

1. 이 좌석은 비상시만을 위한 비상구입니다.

____.

2. 비상구 좌석에 앉아계신 승객들께서는 비상시 승무원을 도와 승객들의 탈출을 도우셔야 합니다.

____.

3. 불안정한 기류관계로 기체가 약간 흔들릴 것으로 예상됩니다.

____.

4. 이륙 준비를 하고 있습니다.

____.

5. 좌석 벨트를 매 주시고, 좌석 등받이와 테이블은 제 자리로 해 주시기 바랍니다.

____.

UNIT

8

In-flight Beverage & Meal Service

기내음료 및 식사 제공하기

Target Skills

1. 객실 서비스 규정에 따라, 비알콜 음료와 알콜 음료에 관한 정보를 승객에게 전달할 수 있다.
2. 객실 서비스 규정에 따라, 승객 선호를 확인하여, 테이블 매너에 따른 기내식을 서비스 할 수 있다.
3. 객실 서비스 규정에 따라, 승객 선호를 확인하여, 음료서비스를 할 수 있다.

Vocabulary Zone

1. meal
2. California
3. Bordeaux
4. prefer
5. available
6. Heineken
7. trash
8. glass

Target Expressions

1. Would you care for some drinks before your meal?: 식사 전 음료 하시겠습니까?
2. We have red wine and white wine from California or Bordeaux.: 캘리포니아산, 혹은 보르도산 레드와인과 화이트 와인이 준비되어 있습니다.
3. Which one would you prefer?: 어느 것으로 하시겠습니까?
4. Excuse me, we are serving dinner.: 실례지만, 저녁 식사 서비스 중입니다.
5. We have a choice of beef steak or chicken with rice.: 쇠고기 스테이크와 닭고기 덮밥이 준비되어 있습니다.
6. I'm sorry, sir. Bibimbap is not available in this flight.: 죄송하지만, 이 구간에서는 비빔밥이 서비스 되지 않습니다.
7. Instead, we have chicken with rice.: 그 대신에 닭고기 덮밥이 준비되어 있습니다.
8. Would you care for a drink with your meal?: 식사와 함께 음료하시겠습니까?
9. Do you need anything else? 그 밖에 필요한 것이 있으십니까?
10. Would you care for coffee?: 커피하시겠습니까?
11. Another flight attendant will serve tea very soon.: 다른 승무원이 곧 차를 서비스하겠습니다.
12. May I have your cup here on the tray?: 이 쟁반에 컵을 올려 주시겠습니까?
13. It might be hot, please be careful.: 뜨거울 수 있으니 조심해 주십시오.

Dialogue 1

Aperitif-Beverage before Meal Service

FA: Flight Attendant

PAX: Passenger

FA : **Would you care for some drinks before your meal?**

PAX : Do you have wine?

FA : **Yes, we have red wine and white wine from California or Bordeaux. Which one would you prefer?**

PAX : I'll have Californian red wine.

FA : Certainly, sir. Here's your red wine.

PAX : Thank you.

FA : You're welcome. Enjoy your flight.

Grammar Drill Zone

1. Would you care for some drinks before your meal?: 식사 전 음료 하시겠습니까?
2. We have red wine and white wine from California or Bordeaux.: 캘리포니아산, 혹은 보르도산 레드와인과 화이트 와인이 준비되어 있습니다.
3. Which one would you prefer?: 어느 것으로 하시겠습니까?

1. Would you care for	some drinks hot towel	before your meal ?
2. We have	red wine and white wine from California or Bordeaux juices, soft drinks, beers, and wine	.
3. Which one would you	prefer care for	?

Practice Zone

: Fill in the blanks to practice in pairs. Take turns to be a flight attendant and a passenger.

Aperitif-Beverage before Meal Service

FA: Flight Attendant

PAX: Passenger

FA : Would you care for some drinks before your (   )?

PAX : Do you have a wine?

FA : Yes, we (   ) red wine and white wine from California or Bordeaux.

(   ) one would you prefer?

PAX : I'll have Californian red wine.

FA : (   ), sir. Here's your red wine.

PAX : Thank you.

FA : You're welcome. Enjoy your flight.

Dialogue 2

Meal Service

FA: Flight Attendant

PAX: Passenger

FA : **Excuse me, we are serving dinner.** Would you please open the tray table?

PAX : Sure. What do you have?

FA : **We have a choice of beef steak or chicken with rice.** Which one would you care for, sir?

PAX : Do you have bibimbap today?

FA : **I'm sorry, sir. Bibimbap is not available in this flight. Instead, we have chicken with rice.**

PAX : OK. I'll take chicken with rice.

FA : Certainly, sir. Here's your Chicken. **Would you care for a drink with your meal?** We have juices, soft drinks, beers and wine.

PAX : Do you have Heineken?

FA : Certainly, sir. Here's your Heineken. **Do you need anything else?**

PAX : No, thanks. It's enough.

FA : Please enjoy your meal.

Grammar Drill Zone

1. Excuse me, we are serving dinner.: 실례지만, 저녁 식사서비스 중입니다.
2. We have a choice of beef steak or chicken with rice.: 쇠고기 스테이크와 닭고기 덮밥이 준비되어 있습니다.
3. I'm sorry, sir. Bibimbap is not available in this flight.: 죄송하지만, 이 구간에서는 비빔밥이 서비스 되지 않습니다.
4. Instead, we have chicken with rice.: 그 대신에 닭고기 덮밥이 준비되어 있습니다.
5. Would you care for a drink with your meal?: 식사와 함께 음료하시겠습니까?
6. Do you need anything else? 그 밖에 필요한 것이 있으십니까?

1. Excuse me, we are serving	dinner	.
	supper	
	lunch	
	breakfast	

2. We have a choice of	beef steak	or	chicken with rice	.
	fried seafood with rice	or	fish with noodle	

3. I'm sorry, sir.	Bibimbap	is not available in this flight.
	Wine	
	Sparkling wine	

4. Instead, we have	chicken with rice	.
	whisky	
	pineapple juice	

5. Would you care for	a drink	with your meal?
	coffee	
	wine	

6. Do you need	anything else	?
	another coffee	
	another wine	

Practice Zone

: Fill in the blanks to practice in pairs. Take turns to be a flight attendant and a passenger.

Meal Service

FA: Flight Attendant

PAX: Passenger

FA : Excuse me, we are (   ) dinner. Would you please open the tray table?

PAX: Sure. What do you have?

FA : We have a (   ) of beef steak or chicken with rice. Which one would you care for, sir?

PAX: Do you have bibimbap today?

FA : I'm sorry, sir. Bibimbap is (   ) (   ) in this flight. (   ), we have chicken with rice.

PAX: OK. I'll take chicken with rice.

FA : Certainly, sir. Here's your Chicken. Would you (   ) (   ) a drink with your meal? We have juices, soft drinks, beers, and wine.

PAX: Do you have Heineken?

FA : Certainly, sir. Here's your Heineken. Do you need anything (   )?

PAX: No, thanks. It's enough.

FA : Please enjoy your meal.

Dialogue 3

Coffee or Tea Service

FA: Flight Attendant

PAX: Passenger

FA : **Would you care for coffee?**

PAX : No, thanks. May I have some tea?

FA : **Another flight attendant will serve tea very soon.** Please wait a moment.

PAX : Let me just have coffee, then.

FA : Certainly, sir. **May I have your cup here on the tray?**

PAX : Here it is.

FA : Thank you. Here's your coffee. **It might be hot, please be careful.**

PAX : Thank you.

FA : Please enjoy your drink.

Grammar Drill Zone

1. Would you care for coffee?: 커피하시겠습니까?
2. Another flight attendant will serve tea very soon.: 다른 승무원이 곧 차를 서비스하겠습니다.
3. May I have your cup here on the tray?: 이 쟁반에 컵을 올려 주시겠습니까?
4. It might be hot, please be careful.: 뜨거울 수 있으니 조심해 주십시오.

1. Would you care for [coffee / tea / wine] ?

2. Another flight attendant will serve [tea / coffee / white wine] very soon.

3. May I have [your cup / your glass / trash] here on the tray?

4. [It might be hot / It is hot] , please be careful.

Practice Zone

: **Fill in the blanks to practice in pairs. Take turns to be a flight attendant and a passenger.**

Coffee or Tea Service

FA: Flight Attendant

PAX: Passenger

FA : Would you ( ) ( ) coffee?

PAX : No, thanks. May I have some tea?

FA : ( ) flight attendant will serve tea very soon. Please wait a moment.

PAX : Let me just have coffee, then.

FA : Certainly, sir. May I have your cup ( ) on the tray?

PAX : Here it is.

FA : Thank you. Here's your coffee. It might be hot, please ( ) ( ).

PAX : Thank you.

FA : Please enjoy your drink.

Reading Comprehension and Discussion

: Read the passage and answer the questions. You may look up the dictionary for words.

What is the nationality of a baby born on an airplane?

A few years ago, a baby was born on the Turkish Airlines flight from West Africa to Burkina Faso. A mother who was on the 28th week of pregnancy suddenly appealed for pain during the flight and gave birth to her daughter with the calm help of the flight attendants. After the airplane landed at an airport in Africa, the mother and baby moved to a local hospital immediately and received a medical examination. A Turkish aviation official said, "We have continued to care for our mothers and babies after landing, and we are all in good health."

By the way, there is argument about the nationality of this baby born at 42,000 feet up in the sky. The nationality of a mother who is an African with French citizenship will have the nationality of France or Africa, but it is a matter to consider in which country the airspace of the baby was born at birth.

The United Nations reported that the baby should follow the nationality of the aircraft on which it was born, which would allow the baby to acquire Turkish nationality, unlike her mother's nationality. What do you think?

* pregnancy: 임신
* suddenly: 갑자기
* appealed: 호소하다
* medical examination: 건강진단
* nationality: 국적
* citizenship: 시민권
* airspace: 영공
* acquire: 획득하다

Q1. According to the passage, where is the final destinaton of this aircraft?

:____.

Q2. According to the passage, what is the nationality of the baby's mother?

:____.

Q3. If the decision of UN is accepted, which nationality will be given to the baby born in the airplane?

:____.

✈ Discussion Topic

If a baby is born in the airplane, which nationality should be given to the baby? Choose one among three examples given below and provide at least two reasons of your opinion.

Example

a. Follow the nationality of the mother

b. Follow the nationality of the airline company.

c. Follow the nationality of the airspace.

: I think the baby's nationality must be given following the

nationality of ______________________________________. I will provide two reasons of my opinion.

First, ____.

Second, ____.

Wrap Up Activity

Match the word and the right definition.

1. meal
2. California
3. Bordeaux
4. prefer
5. available
6. Heineken
7. trash
8. glass

a. A major center of the wine in France.

b. Such as window and bottles.

c. The food you eat normally three times a day.

d. Unwanted things or waste.

e. When you can find and obtain something or someone.

f. A beer first made in Netherlands.

g. Similar meaning of like in verb.

h. A state on the west coast of the US.

Exercise

1–5. Please translate the sentences into English.

1. 쇠고기 스테이크와 닭고기 덮밥이 준비되어 있습니다.

____.

2. 죄송하지만, 이 구간에서는 비빔밥이 서비스 되지 않습니다.

____.

3. 그 대신에 생선 덮밥이 준비되어 있습니다.

____.

4. 컵을 이 곳 쟁반에 올려 주시겠습니까?

____.

5. 뜨거울 수 있으니 주의해 주십시오.

____.

UNIT

9

In-flight Duty Free Sales

기내 면세품 판매하기

Target Skills

1. 객실 서비스 규정에 따라 기내 면세품 판매를 위한 기본적인 상품을 안내하고 판매할 수 있다.
2. 객실 서비스 규정에 따라 면세품 판매를 위한 지불 가능 화폐와 방법을 안내하고 판매할 수 있다.
3. 객실 서비스 규정에 따라 품절된 상품을 안내하고 다른 상품을 추천하여 면세품을 판매할 수 있다.

Vocabulary Zone

1. duty-free
2. items
3. goods
4. iquors,
5. perfumes
6. cosmetics
7. chocolates
8. gift items
9. credit card
10. cash
11. double check

Target Expressions

1. Would you like to purchase duty-free items?: 면세품 주문하시겠습니까?
2. We have liquors, perfumes, cosmetics, chocolates and gift items.: 면세품으로는 술, 향수, 화장품, 초콜릿 그리고 선물용 제품들이 있습니다.
3. How would you like to pay, by credit or cash?: 지불화폐는 카드로 하시겠습니까? 아니면 현금으로 하시겠습니까?
4. Here's your perfume and the receipt. Please double check your order.: 여기 향수와 영수증입니다. 주문을 다시 한번 확인해 주십시오.
5. May I take your order, sir?: 주문하시겠습니까?
6. I'm terribly sorry, sir. It has been sold out.: 대단히 죄송하지만, 그 제품은 품절되었습니다.

Dialogue 1

Duty Free Sales 1

: General

FA: Flight Attendant

PAX: Passenger

FA : We are selling duty-free items. **Would you like to purchase duty-free items?**

PAX : Yes. What do you have?

FA : **We have liquors, perfumes, cosmetics, chocolates and gift items.** What would you like, sir?

PAX : What kinds of perfume do you have?

FA : We have Chanel, Christian Dior, Prada and Bvlgari.

PAX : Let me have Chanel, please.

FA : Certainly, sir. **How would you like to pay, by credit or cash?**

PAX : I'll pay by credit card.

FA : Certainly, sir. May I have your credit card? Let me get your perfume as soon as possible.

(After a while. FA comes back with a perfume and receipt.)

FA : Thank you for waiting, sir. **Here's your perfume and the receipt. Please double check your order.** It's $35 by credit card.

PAX : That's right. Thank you.

FA : It's my pleasure.

Grammar Drill Zone

1. Would you like to purchase duty-free items?: 면세품 주문하시겠습니까?
2. We have liquors, perfumes, cosmetics, chocolates and gift items.: 면세품으로는 술, 향수, 화장품, 초콜릿 그리고 선물용 제품들이 있습니다.
3. How would you like to pay, by credit or cash?: 지불화폐는 카드로 하시겠습니까? 아니면 현금으로 하시겠습니까?
4. Here's your perfume and the receipt. Please double check your order.: 여기 향수와 영수증입니다. 주문을 다시 한번 확인해 주십시오.

1. Would you like to purchase duty-free [items / goods / gift items]?

2. We have [liquors, perfumes, cosmetics, chocolates and gift items / cosmetics, various gift items and wines for sale].

3. How would you like to pay, [by credit or cash / Korean won or USD]?

4. Here's your [perfume / order] and the receipt. Please double check [your order / item].

Practice Zone

: **Fill in the blanks to practice in pairs. Take turns to be a flight attendant and a passenger.**

Duty Free Sales 1

: ***General***

FA: Flight Attendant

PAX: Passenger

FA : We are selling ( )-( ) items. Would you like to purchase ( )-( ) items?

PAX : Yes. What do you have?

FA : We ( ) liquors, perfumes, cosmetics, chocolates and gift items. What would you ( ), sir?

PAX : What kinds of perfume do you have?

FA : We have Chanel, Christian Dior, Prada and Bvlgari.

PAX : Let me have Chanel, please.

FA : Certainly, sir. How would you like to(   ), by (   ) or cash?

PAX : I'll pay by credit card.

FA : Certainly, sir. May I have your credit card? Let me get your perfume as (   ) as possible.

(After a while. FA comes back with a perfume and receipt.)

FA : Thank you for (   ), sir. Here's your perfume and the receipt. Please (   ) check your order. It's $35 by credit card.

PAX : That's right. Thank you.

FA : It's my pleasure.

Dialogue 2

Duty Free Sales 2

: Sold Out Items

FA: Flight Attendant

PAX: Passenger

PAX: (PAX Call rings.)

FA : Thank you for waiting. **May I take your order, sir?**

PAX: I'd like to buy a set of Lancome lipsticks.

FA : **I'm terribly sorry, sir. It has been sold out.** Instead, we have a set of Chanel lipstics and Christian Dior lip glosses. Would care for one of them?

PAX: Yes, I'll buy a set of Christian Dior lip gloss, please.

FA : Certainly, sir. That will be $ 50.

PAX: All right, I'll pay by USD.

FA : Certainly, sir. Please wait a moment.

Grammar Drill Zone

1. May I take your order, sir?: 주문하시겠습니까?
2. I'm terribly sorry, sir. It has been sold out.: 대단히 죄송하지만, 그 제품은 품절되었습니다.

1.	May I take your Are you ready to	order, sir?
2. I'm terribly sorry, sir. It	has been sold out is not available in this flight	.

Practice Zone

: Fill in the blanks to practice in pairs. Take turns to be a flight attendant and a passenger.

Duty Free Sales 2

: Sold Out Items

FA: Flight Attendant

PAX: Passenger

PAX : (PAX Call rings.)

FA : Thank you for waiting. May I take your (   ), sir?

PAX : I'd like to buy a set of Lancome lipsticks.

FA : I'm terribly sorry, sir. It has been (   ) (   ). Instead, we have a set of Chanel lipstics and Christian Dior lip glosses. Would (   ) for one of them?

PAX : Yes, I'll buy a set of Christian Dior lip gloss, please.

FA : Certainly, sir. That will be $ 50.

PAX : All right, I'll pay by USD.

FA : Certainly, sir. Please wait a (   ).

Reading Comprehension

: Read and compare the duty-free allowances of countries.

"Duty Free allowances for Korea and Other Countries"

√ **Country**

Alcohol/ Tobacco

√ Australia

2.25 litres alcoholic beverage/ 25 cigarettes or 25 grams tobacco

√ Canada

1 litre alcoholic beverage/ 200 cigarettes or 50 cigars

√ China

1.5 litres alcoholic beverage/ 400 cigarettes

√ Fiji

4.5 litres wine or beer or 2.25 litres spirits or liqueur/ 250 cigarettes or 250 grams tobacco or 250 grams cigars

√ Hong Kong

1 litre of alcohol/ 19 cigarettes or 25 grams of tobacco or 25 grams of cigars

√ Japan

3x 750ml of alcoholic beverage/

Residents: 200 cigarettes

Non-residents: 400 cigarettes or 250 grams tobacco

√ South Korea

1 litre of alcohol/ 200 cigarettes or 50 cigars

√ Malaysia

1 litre of alcohol/ 200 cigarettes or 50 cigars or 225 grams tobacco

√ New Caledonia

2 litres of spirits except Aniseed or Absinthe and 2 litres of wine/ 200 cigarettes or 100 cigarillos or 50 cigars or 400 grams tobacco

√ New Zealand

Up to 3 litres of spirits or liqueur (conditions apply) plus 6 bottles of wine, port or sherry/ 50 cigarettes or 50 grams cigars or 50 grams tobacco

√ Norfolk Island

1 litre alcoholic beverage/ 200 cigarettes or 250 grams tobacco/cigars

√ Samoa

2.25 litres of alcohol/ 200 cigarettes or 250 grams of tobacco/cigars

√ Singapore

1 litre spirits and 1 litre wine or beer/ No cigarettes, all tobacco goods must be declared

√ South Africa

2 litres wine and 1 litre spirits/ 400 cigarettes and 250 grams tobacco and 50 cigars

√ Taiwan

1 litre of alcohol/ 200 cigarettes or 25 cigars or 500 grams of tobacco

√ Thailand

1 litre of alcohol/ 200 cigarettes or 250 grams of tobacco or equal weight of cigars

√ Tonga

2.25 litres of spirits or 4.5 litres of wine/ 400 cigarettes or 500 grams of tobacco/cigars

√ United Kingdom

2 litres wine and 1 litre spirits/ 200 cigarettes or 50 cigars or 100 cigarillos or 250 grams tobacco

√ United States of America

1 litre alcoholic beverage/ 200 cigarettes or 50 cigars or 1,350 gms tobacco

or combination

*Cuban cigars are not permitted to be imported

√ Vanuatu

2 litres wine and 1.5 litres spirits/ 200 cigarettes or 50 cigars or 250 grams tobacco

- * alcohol: 술
- * spirit: 주류
- * tobacco: 담배
- * cigarette: 담배
- * permitted: 허가된

Q1. How many liters of wine and spirits does South Korea allow?

:______________________________

Q2. Which country doesn't allow Cuban cigars?

:______________________________

Q3. There is a country never allows any cigarette, which country is it?

:______________________________

✈ Discussion Topic

1. Why do we have duty-free allowance?

:____

____.

2. Do you think the amount of duty-free allowances for your country is appropriate or inappropriate? Why?

:____

____

____

____

____

____.

Wrap Up Activity

Word Search

S D U T Y E Q S Y C C Y I F L
R E Z Y M G E C P L R H B L F
N E T Z A M U I M F K E P D Y
G M Q A U N Q T D L X B D F O
W T Z F L W E E J O Y R X I D
C Z R D T O M M R U E Y J I T
V E N O I Z C S V Z U H T Q S
P G C U C Y Q O W L H S N J J
F Z X B W Q I C H S T F I G S
G B P L B T T K H C H Z J P M
W P Q E C U S M N X F B R X E
T X Z H P A G D O E D G H P T
H H E G L I Q U O R S S T S I
B C B W C T K P T O A P W Q O
K P T K K A B C R C G I U D G

CASH
CHECK
CHOCOLATES
COSMETICS
CREDIT
DOUBLE
DUTY
GIFTS
GOODS
ITEMS
LIQUORS
PERFUMES

Exercise

1–5. Please translate the sentences into English.

1. 면세품 주문하시겠습니까?

____.

2. 면세품으로는 술, 향수, 화장품, 초콜릿 그리고 선물용 제품들이 있습니다.

____.

3. 지불화폐는 카드로 하시겠습니까? 아니면 현금으로 하시겠습니까?

____.

4. 여기 술과 영수증입니다. 주문을 다시 한번 확인해 주십시오.

____.

5. 대단히 죄송하지만, 그 제품은 품절되었습니다.

____.

UNIT

10

Handling Complaints

불만 승객 대처하기

Target Skills

1. 객실 서비스 및 객실 안전 규정에 따라 불만 상황에 대한 원인을 파악할 수 있다.
2. 객실 서비스 및 안전 규정에 따라 경청한 후 불만에 대한 해결 방안을 모색할 수 있다.
3. 객실 서비스 및 안전 규정에 따라 해결 방안에 대한 구체적인 행동을 보여줄 수 있다.
4. 객실 서비스 규정에 따라 해당 승객의 기내 서비스 만족도를 재확인할 수 있다.

Vocabulary Zone

1. vegetarian
2. on board
3. sodium
4. apology
5. accept
6. assorted
7. appreciate
8. delivery
9. aviation
10. patience

Target Expressions

1. Let me go and check as soon as possible.: 제가 가서 최대한 빠르게 확인해보겠습니다.
2. I'm really sorry, sir. Your vegetarian meal is not on board.: 손님, 대단히 죄송합니다. 채식 식사가 탑재되지 않았습니다.
3. There may have been a mistake in reservation.: 예약 과정에 문제가 있었던 것 같습니다.
4. Please accept our apology.: 저희의 사과를 받아주십시오.
5. We appreciate your understanding.: 양해해 주셔서 감사합니다.
6. While you're waiting, would you like some hot drinks?: 기다리시는 동안 뜨거운 음료 하시겠습니까?
7. I hope you'll get well soon.: 금방 회복되시길 바랍니다.

Dialogue 1

Complaints–Meal Service

FA: Flight Attendant

PAX: Passenger

PAX : Let me have my vegetarian meal, please.

FA : Could I have your name and seat number, sir?

PAX : Collin Dicaprio in 24D.

FA : Would you please wait a mement? **Let me go and check as soon as possible.**

PAX : Sure.

(After a while.)

FA : **I'm really sorry, sir. Your vegetarian meal is not on board.** And I can't find your name in our special meal list, either. **There may have been a mistake in reservation.**

PAX : I don't understand this airline staffs. I can't eat any other food but vegetable. Do I have to wait another 8 hours until I land on the airport?

FA : **Please accept our apology.** Let me check if there's what I can do. Please wait a moment.

(FA goes to galley and comes back in a moment.)

FA : I'm very sorry to have kept you waiting, sir. We serve assorted cheese and fruit in this flight in other class. I've heard that one of them is available. Would you like to try, sir?

PAX : Well, yes, if there's no other choice.

FA : **We appreciate your understanding.** Here they are. If you need anything else, please let us know.

Grammar Drill Zone

Complaints-Meal Service

1. Let me go and check as soon as possible.: 제가 가서 최대한 빠르게 확인해보겠습니다.
2. I'm really sorry, sir. Your vegetarian meal is not on board.: 손님, 대단히 죄송합니다. 채식 식사가 탑재되지 않았습니다.
3. There may have been a mistake in reservation.: 예약과정에 문제가 있었던 것 같습니다.
4. Please accept our apology.: 저희의 사과를 받아주십시오.
5. We appreciate your understanding.: 양해해 주셔서 감사합니다.

1. Let me go and check	as soon as possible right away immediately	.
2. I'm really sorry, sir. Your	vegetarian meal child meal low sodium meal	is not on board.
3. There may have been a mistake in	reservation seat arrangement delivery	.
4. Please accept	our apology aviation law	.
5. We appreciate your	understanding patience	.

Practice Zone

: Fill in the blanks to practice in pairs. Take turns to be a flight attendant and a passenger.

Complaints–Meal Service

FA: Flight Attendant

PAX: Passenger

PAX : Let me have my vegetarian meal, please.

FA : Could I have your ( ) and seat number, sir?

PAX : Collin Dicaprio in 24D.

FA : Would you please wait a mement? Let me go and check ( ) ( ) ( ) possible.

PAX : Sure.

(After a while.)

FA : I'm really sorry, sir. Your vegetarian meal is not ( ) ( ). And I can't find your name in our special meal ( ), either.

There may have been a (　　　　) in reservation.

PAX : I don't understand this airline staffs. I can't eat any other food but vegetable. Do I have to wait another 8 hours until I land on the airport?

FA : Please accept our (　　　　). Let me check if there's what I can do. Please wait a moment.
(FA goes to galley and comes back in a moment.)

FA : I'm very sorry to have kept you (　　　　), sir. We serve assorted cheese and fruit in this flight in other class. I've heard that one of them is (　　　　). Would you like to (　　　　), sir?

PAX : Well, yes, if there's no other choice.

FA : We (　　　　) your understanding. Here they are. If you need anything else, please let us know.

Dialogue 2

Complaints–Cabin Condition

FA: Flight Attendant

PAX: Passenger

(PAX Call rings.)

FA : May I help you, sir?

PAX : Yes, it's so cold.

FA : May I get you another blanket, sir?

PAX : No, thanks. It doen't help.

FA : I'm sorry, sir. Let me check the cabin temperature. **While you're waiting, would you like some hot drinks?**

PAX : Sounds good. May I have a cup of hot tea?

FA : Certainly, sir. Please wait a second.

(After a while, FA comes back.)

FA : Thank you for waiting, sir. Here's your tea. Please becareful, it might be hot.
And I slightly raised cabin temperature. **I hope you'll get well soon.**

PAX : Thanks. That's very kind of you.

FA : It's my pleasure. If you need any help, please let us know.

Grammar Drill Zone

1. While you're waiting, would you like some hot drinks?: 기다리시는 동안 뜨거운 음료 하시겠습니까?
2. I hope you'll get well soon.: 금방 회복되시길 바랍니다.

1. While you're waiting, would you like	some hot drinks something to read	?
2. I hope you'll	get well soon recover quikly	.

Practice Zone

: Fill in the blanks to practice in pairs. Take turns to be a flight attendant and a passenger.

Complaints–Cabin Condition

FA: Flight Attendant

PAX: Passenger

(PAX Call rings.)

FA : May I help you, sir?

PAX : Yes, it's so cold.

FA : May I (   ) you another blanket, sir?

PAX : No, thanks. It doen't help.

FA : I'm sorry, sir. Let me check the cabin (   ).
(   ) you're waiting, would you like some hot drinks?

PAX : Sounds good. May I have a cup of hot tea?

FA : (   ), sir. Please wait a second.

(After a while, FA comes back.)

FA : Thank you for waiting, sir. Here's your tea. Please becareful, it might be hot.

And I slightly raised cabin temperature. I hope you'll (   ) (   ) soon.

PAX : Thanks. That's very kind of you.

FA : It's my pleasure. If you need any (   ), please let us know.

Reading Comprehension and Discussion

: Read the passage and answer the questions. You may look up the dictionary for words.

5-process principle responding passenger complaints.

1. Stop to listen carefully.

   When a customer presents you with a complaint, carefully listen and try to empathize with the passenger. Let the passenger know that you are truely caring.

2. Aplogize sincerely.

   Apologize first for any inconviences even though it is vague to find the fault of yours.

3. Provide solution.

   If there is not any best solution, try to find the second best solution.

4. Check the satisfaction.

   During the rest of the flight time, keep on eye on the passenger not to commit the same mistake by sharing information of the case with other crew members.

5. Report the case.

It is difficult to blame on the crew member who dealt with the complaits sincerely and appropriately even if how hot the complaints might had been. Also the case can be shared and gathered for filing the passenger satisfaction information.

* present: 표현하다
* complaint: 불만
* empathize: 공감하다
* sincerely: 진심으로
* solution: 해결책
* commit: 저지르다
* blarne: 비난하다
* dealt: (deal의 과거형) 처리했다
* appropriately: 적당하게, 알맞게

Q1. What is the next step of careful listening?

: ______________________________

Q2. When is the best time to apologize? Circle the most appropriate answer.

① As soon as possible

② After you listen carefully.

③ After you investigate the situation carefully.

④ When you can understand the passenger completely.

✈ Discussion Topic

"Have you ever apologized even if you didn't feel sorry?"

1. When?

:

2. Where?

:

3. What happened?

:

4. How did you feel after apology?

:

5. What if you didn't apologize?

Wrap Up Activity

Word & Definition

:Write your own definition of the following words.

1. *vegetarian* is someone who doesn't ______________________________.

2. *on board* means where you are in ______________________________.

3. *sodium* is similar to ______________________________.

4. *apology* is something you do when you ______________________________.

5. *accept* means that you ______________________________.

6. *assorted* chocolates, chesses, ______________, ______________ are my favorites.

7. *appreciate* can be also used in gallery when you see ______________.

8. *delivery* means brining duty free order items to ______________________.

9. *aviation* service industry is the field where I ______________________.

10. *patience* is the best value you can learn from ______________________.

Exercise

1–5. Please translate the sentences into English.

1. 제가 가서 최대한 빠르게 확인해보겠습니다.

____.

2. 손님, 대단히 죄송합니다만, 어린이용 식사가 탑재되지 않았습니다.

____.

3. 저희의 사과를 받아주십시오.

____.

4. 기다리시는 동안 차가운 음료 하시겠습니까?

____.

5. 금방 회복되시길 바랍니다.

____.

PART

4

Before Landing
착륙전 서비스

UNIT

11

Preparing for Landing

착륙 준비하기

Target Skills

1. 객실 서비스 규정에 따라 하기하는 데 특별한 조치가 필요한 승객에 대해 확인하고 선임자에게 보고할 수 있다.
2. 객실 안전 규정에 따라 의심스러운 승객 또는 불만 승객에 대한 상황 처리 결과를 선임자에게 보고할 수 있다.
3. 객실 서비스 규정에 따라, 서비스 아이템에 대한 회수를 진행하고 적절한 곳에 보관하여 인수인계 할 수 있다.

Vocabulary Zone

1. wheelchair
2. deplane
3. arrival
4. UM(Unacompanied Minor)
5. recognize
6. estimated
7. local
8. collection
9. pleasant

Target Expressions

1. Did you order a wheelchair at the arrival airport?: 도착 공항에 휠체어를 주문하셨습니까?
2. Would you like to deplane first or later?: 먼저 내리시겠습니까, 나중에 내리시겠습니까?
3. Did you have a good rest?: 편히 쉬셨습니까?
4. Let me guide you to one of our ground staffs waiting at the arrival airport.: 제가 도착 공항에서 기다리고 있는 저희 직원중 한 명에게 모셔다 드리겠습니다.
5. We are landing shortly.: 곧 착륙하겠습니다.
6. Estimated arrival time is 11:05 am. in local time.: 도착 예정 시간은 현지 시간으로 오전 11시 5분 입니다.

Dialogue 1

Special Passenger Care–Wheelchair

FA: Flight Attendant

PAX: Passenger

FA : Excuse me, sir. **Did you order a wheelchair at the arrival airport?**

PAX : Yes, I did.

FA : **Would you like to deplane first or later?**

PAX : First, please.

FA : Certainly, sir. Let us prepare a wheelchair at the door when you deplane first.

PAX : Thank you.

FA : Have a nice stay, sir.

Grammar Drill Zone

1. Did you order a wheelchair at the arrival airport?: 도착 공항에 휠체어를 주문하셨습니까?
2. Would you like to deplane first or later?: 먼저 내리시겠습니까, 나중에 내리시겠습니까?

1.	Did you order Shall I prepare	a wheelchair at the arrival airport?

2. Would you like to	deplane first or later wait in your seat until I come to you	?

Practice Zone

: Fill in the blanks to practice in pairs. Take turns to be a flight attendant and a passenger.

Special Passenger Care–Wheelchair

FA: Flight Attendant

PAX: Passenger

FA : Excuse me, sir. Did you order a wheelchair at the (   ) airport?

PAX : Yes, I did.

FA : Would you like to (   ) first or later?

PAX : First, please.

FA : (   ), sir. Let us prepare a wheelchair at the door when you deplane first.

PAX : Thank you.

FA : Have a nice stay, sir.

Dialogue 2

Special Passenger Care–UM

FA: Flight Attendant

PAX: Passenger

FA : Excuse me. **Did you have a good rest?** When we land, please wait in your seat untill I come to you. **Let me guide you to one of our ground staffs waiting at the arrival airport.**

PAX : Yes, I will. Thank you.

FA : Please wear your UM tag so we can recognize you well.

PAX : Sure. No problem.

FA : Thank you very much.

Grammar Drill Zone

1. Did you have a good rest?: 편히 쉬셨습니까?
2. Let me guide you to one of our ground staffs waiting at the arrival airport.: 제가 도착 공항에서 기다리고 있는 저희 직원중 한 명에게 모셔다 드리겠습니다.

1. Did you have a good trip / stay ?

2. Let me guide / report you to one of our ground staffs waiting at the arrival airport.

Practice Zone

: Fill in the blanks to practice in pairs. Take turns to be a flight attendant and a passenger.

Special Passenger Care-UM

FA: Flight Attendant

PAX: Passenger

FA : Excuse me. Did you (   ) a good trip? When we (   ), please wait in your seat untill I come to you. Let me guide you to one of our (   ) (   ) waiting at the arrival airport.

PAX : Yes, I will. Thank you.

FA : Please wear your UM tag so we can (   ) you well.

PAX : Sure. No problem.

FA : Thank you very much.

Dialogue 3

Collection of Service Items

FA: Flight Attendant

PAX: Passenger

FA : Did you have a good rest, sir? **We are landing shortly.** May I have your headphone?

PAX : Here you are. What time is the arrival?

FA : **Estimated arrival time is 11:05 am. in local time.** We have 15 minutes left. Please return your seat back and tray table.

PAX : Sure.

FA : Thank you. I hope you have a pleasant stay.

Grammar Drill Zone

1. We are landing shortly.: 곧 착륙하겠습니다.
2. Estimated arrival time is 11:05 am. in local time.: 도착 예정 시간은 현지 시간으로 오전 11시 5분 입니다.

1. We are [landing shortly / arriving soon].

2. Estimated [arrival / departure] time is [11:05 am. / 10:30 pm.] in local time.

Practice Zone

: Fill in the blanks to practice in pairs. Take turns to be a flight attendant and a passenger.

Collection of Service Items

FA: Flight Attendant

PAX: Passenger

FA : Did you have a good rest, sir? We are landing (   ). May I have your headphone?

PAX : Here you are. What (   ) is the arrival?

FA : (   ) arrival time is 11:05 am. in local time. We have 15 minutes left. Please return your (   ) (   ) and tray table.

PAX : Sure.

FA : Thank you. I hope you have a pleasant (   ).

Wrap Up Activity

Unscramble the Word

① edelanp ________

② hweelcairh ___________

③ varialr ________

④ duern inomr ______ ______

⑤ neorgizec __________

⑥ mestiadte __________

⑦ clola ______

⑧ nctoleciol ___________

⑨ nleapsat _________

Exercise

1–5. Please translate the sentences into English.

1. 도착 공항에 휠체어를 주문하셨습니까?

____.

2. 먼저 내리시겠습니까, 나중에 내리시겠습니까?

____.

3. 제가 도착 공항에서 기다리고 있는 저희 직원중 한 명에게 모셔다 드리겠습니다.

____.

4. 편히 쉬셨습니까?

____.

5. 도착 예정 시간은 현지 시간으로 오후 10시 25분 입니다.

____.

UNIT

12

Entry Documents

입국 서류 작성 지원하기

Target Skills

1. 객실 서비스 규정에 따라 도착지 국가별 요구사항에 따른 서류를 안내하고 배포할 수 있다.
2. 객실 서비스 규정에 따라 국가별 면세 허용량에 따른 반입 가능 금액을 안내하며 세관 서류 작성을 도울 수 있다.
3. 객실 서비스 규정에 따라 항공기 도착 전 해당 국가의 입국서류 작성을 도울 수 있다.

Vocabulary Zone

1. entry
2. document
3. nationality
4. arrival card
5. customs declaration form
6. except
7. transit
8. fill out
9. foreigners
10. citizen
11. resident
12. product
13. quarantine
14. liquid
15. aviation

Target Expressions

1. Please have your passport and other entry documents ready.: 여권과 다른 입국서류를 준비해 주십시오.
2. All foreigners entering into Korea, must fill out the arrival card.: 한국에 입국하시는 모든 외국인 손님께서는 입국신고서를 작성하셔야 합니다.
3. Do you want me to help you with the arrival card?: 입국 신고서 작성에 도움이 필요하십니까?
4. All passengers must fill out the customs declaration form.: 모든 손님께서는 세관신고서를 작성하셔야 합니다.
5. Only one form is needed for family members traveling together.: 가족당 한 매만 작성하시면 됩니다.
6. Here's a customs form that is written in English. 여기 영어로 된 세관신고서를 드리겠습니다.

Documentation Announcement

FA: Flight Attendant

FA: Ladies and gentlemen, for entry into Korea, **please have your passport and other entry documents ready.** All passengers except Korean citizens and residents are required to fill out the arrival card. The customs form must be completed by all passengers, however only one is needed for family memebers traveling together. Passengers who have baggage arriving on another aircraft or by ship are required to fill out two customs forms. Also, if you are carrying fruit, plant or meat products from USA, they must be declared to the Animal and Plant Quarantine service office. According to Aviation Security Regulations, passengers transiting to international flights, who have liquid amounts of under 100 mls must put their liquid items inside a clear zip-lock bag. Thank you.

Dialogue 1

Arrival Card

FA: Flight Attendant

PAX: Passenger

PAX : Excuse me, I'll be staying in Korea for 3 days. Do I need an arrival card?

FA : Yes, you do, sir. **All foreigners entering into Korea, must fill out the arrival card.** Here it is, sir.

PAX : Thank you.

FA : **Do you want me to help you with the arrival card?**

PAX : No thanks.

FA : If you need any help, please let us know.

Grammar Drill Zone

1. Please have your passport and other entry documents ready.: 여권과 다른 입국서류를 준비해 주십시오.
2. All foreigners entering into Korea, must fill out the arrival card.: 한국에 입국하시는 모든 외국인 손님께서는 입국신고서를 작성하셔야 합니다.
3. Do you want me to help you with the arrival card?: 입국 신고서 작성에 도움이 필요하십니까?

1. Please have your passport and	other entry documents customs form	ready.
2. All foreigners	entering into Korea except transit passesgers	, must fill out the arrival card.
3. Do you	want me to help you need any help	with the arrival card?

Practice Zone

: Fill in the blanks to practice in pairs. Take turns to be a flight attendant and a passenger.

Arrival Card

FA: Flight Attendant

PAX: Passenger

PAX : Excuse me, I'll be staying in Korea for 3 days. Do I need an arrival card?

FA : Yes, you do, sir. All (   ) entering into Korea, must fill out the arrival card. Here it is, sir.

PAX : Thank you.

FA : Do you want me to help you (   ) the arrival card?

PAX : No thanks.

FA : If you need any help, please let us (   ).

Dialogue 2

Customs Declaration Form

FA: Flight Attendant

PAX: Passenger

FA : Excuse me. Here's customs declaration form. **All passengers must fill out the customs declaration form.**

PAX : All right. May I have three more because there are four members in my family.

FA : Sir, **only one form is needed for family members traveling together.**

PAX : I see......um.....May I have a form that is wriiten in English, please?

FA : Oh, I'm sorry, sir. Let me get you an English form. Please wait a second.

PAX : Thank you for waiting, sir. **Here's a customs form that is written in English.**

FA : Thanks. Oh, I made a mistake. Can I have another form, please?

PAX : Certainly, sir. Here it is. If you need any help, please let us know.

Grammar Drill Zone

1. All apssengers must fill out the customs declaration form.: 모든 손님께서는 세관신고서를 작성하셔야 합니다.
2. Only one form is needed for family members traveling together.: 가족당 한 매만 작성하시면 됩니다.
3. Here's a customs form that is written in English. 여기 영어로 된 세관신고서를 드리겠습니다.

1. All apssengers must fill out the	customs declaration form	.
	aarival card	

2. Only one form is	needed for family members traveling together	.
	per one family	

3. Here's	a customs form	that is written in	English	.
	an arrival card		Korean	

Practice Zone

: Fill in the blanks to practice in pairs. Take turns to be a flight attendant and a passenger.

Customs Declaration Form

FA: Flight Attendant

PAX: Passenger

FA : Excuse me. Here's customs declaration form. All passengers must fill out the customs (   ) form.

PAX : All right. May I have three more forms because there are four members in my family.

FA : Sir, only (   ) form is needed for family members traveling together.

PAX : I see......um.....May I have a form that is written in English, please?

FA : Oh, I'm sorry, sir. Let me get you an English form. Please wait a second.

PAX : Thank you for waiting, sir. Here's a customs form that (   ) (   ) in English.

FA : Thanks. Oh, I made a mistake. Can I have another form, please?

PAX : Certainly, sir. Here it is. If you need any help, please let us (   ).

Practice Zone

: **Fill in the blanks with your partner.**

Documentation Announcement

FA: Flight Attendant

🔔 FA: Ladies and gentlemen, for entry into Korea, please have your passport and other entry d________ ready. All passengers e________ Korean citizens and residents are required to fill out the arrival card. The c________ form must be completed by all passengers, however only o________ is needed for family memebers traveling together. Passengers who have baggage arriving on another aircraft or by ship are required to fill out t________ customs forms. Also, if you are carrying fruit, plant or meat products from USA, they must be declared to the Animal and Plant Quarantine service office. According to Aviation Security Regulations, passengers transiting to international flights, who have liquid amounts of under 100 mls must put their liquid items inside a clear zip-lock bag. Thank you.

Reading Comprehension

: Read the passage and answer the questions. You may look up the dictionary for words.

What you should never do to pass immigration procedure.

First, it is recommended to have eye contact with the examiner during the immigration process. Most western cultures consider it important to face their own eyes to the other's eyes. If you are too nervous to react naturally and show a bad attitude, you should be careful because it can lead to bad results. Sometimes the examiner makes jokes or asks routine questions, but it is better to answer with short words rather than long answers to avoid miscommunication.

Second, vague answers or words should be avoided. A word 'maybe' is a good example. When asked, "What are you here for?" or "What are you going to do?", answering "I think I'm going to travel." is not appropriate. The possibility of illegal residency can be doubted as the examiner feels uncertain. After all, interviews will be prolonged and if you are not fluent in English or foreign languages, you will get twisted. For this reason, it is important to use or express the exact words.

Finally, it's the best to answer only when you understand the question. It can be embarrassing to answer 'yes' or 'no' without understanding the examiner's question properly. If you say 'yes' when the examiner asks if you have any plan to work while you are there, problems become complicated. This is because you wrote 'travel' on your arrival card and responded that you might work there. If you did not understand the question correctly, it would be wise to express your intention such as "I didn't understand well." and "Please ask me questions." Or it's a good idea to ask for an interpreter who can speak Korean.

* recommended: 추천되는
* examiner: 조사관
* vague: 애매한
* possibility: 가능성
* residency: 거주
* uncertain: 불확실한
* complicated: 복잡한
* immigration: 이민국
* routine: 일상적인
* avoid: 피하다
* illegal: 불법의
* doubted: 의심받는
* embarassing: 난처한
* interpreter: 통역자

Q1. Why do we have to use exact words to answer during the immigration procedure?

: ____

____

____.

Q2. According to this article, circle the questions that examiners may ask.

ⓐ When did you get married?

ⓑ What' your plan here?

ⓒ What's the purpose of your visit?

ⓓ When is your birth of date?

ⓔ Why are you here for?

Q3. To sum up, what are the three things we have to do to pass the immigration procedure.

:

1. Have ______________________________.

2. Avoid ______________________________.

3. Answer ______________________________.

✈ Discussion Topic

If you are an examiner of immigration, what kind of questions will you ask to the following people. Think about at least 3 questions for each person.

√Person 1: Pregnant lady with foreign passport.

√Person 2: Gentleman has been denied entry last year.

√Person 3: 25-year-old man graduated university last month.

√Person 1

1.____.

2.____.

3.____.

√Person 2

1.____.

2.____.

3.____.

√Person 3

1.____.

2.____.

3.____.

Wrap Up Activity

Word Search

```
E R G H Z X R T T L Y Y M N T B E X J J
R K D L L N W F J T B M Y O Q P E T M N
M I T W Z G V N I W C M S I A X E Y Y M
T O M Z D G H L D U C P T T C M Y C R H
B N I B M K A L S S U Y R A I T V O X R
F Z L D I N O T O N F B R R T K F Y B E
M X Y A O T O Q A C Y B C A I D G F U Y
N U C I R M J Q O P J H R L Z E F K V S
X J T Y S R J B X H O Y Z C E I Z O Z G
A A I C P C I X E E Y Y Y E N R D B Q Q
N L A K L Z X V F U R W U D D O F E I R
G Y I O T I S N A R T W L C Z V C P F K
D O C U M E N T B L N E K C J C G Y A C
X O T H A X N R I E E U F A O L T V Y W
Y E H Z L K M Y J Q J W W K H V J B H D
```

ARRIVAL
CITIZEN
CUSTOMS
DECLARATION
DOCUMENT
ENTRY
EXCEPT
FORM
NATIONALITY
TRANSIT

Exercise

1–5. Please translate the sentences into English.

1. 여권과 다른 입국서류를 준비해 주십시오.

____.

2. 짐을 다른 항공편이나 배로 부치신 손님께서는 세관신고서 2장을 작성하셔야 합니다.

____.

3. 세관 신고서 작성에 도움이 필요하십니까?

____.

4. 한국에 입국하시는 모든 외국인 손님께서는 입국신고서를 작성하셔야 합니다.

____.

5. 여기 영어로 된 세관신고서를 드리겠습니다.

____.

PART

5

After Landing

착륙후 서비스

Unit 13. Welcome & Farewell Announcement

환영 & 도착 안내 방송하기

UNIT 13

Welcome & Farewell Announcement

환영 & 도착 안내 방송하기

Target Skills

1. 객실 서비스 규정에 따라 항공기 착륙후 목적지 도착 안내 방송을 실시할 수 있다.
2. 객실 서비스 규정에 따라 항공기 착륙후 서비스 안내를 할 수 있다.
3. 객실 서비스 규정에 따라 감사한 마음을 정중하고 명료한 목적지 도착 안내 방송으로 전달할 수 있다.

Vocabulary Zone

destination	atmosphere
announcement	belongings
parsing	intonation
pronunciation	refrain
appreciate	express
connection	entire
contents	patience
feature	assist
departure	permit
electronic device	laptop

✈ How to make a good in-flight announcement.

When you make an announcement, you have to focus on delivering the flight information clearly such as the flight number, flight time, destination, sir name of captain and where the passengers can stow their belongings. Moreover, welcoming and caring atmosphere should also be made carefully. To make a clear announcement, parsing, intonation, pronunciation are the key features.

Welcome Announcement

: Listen to the welcome announcement and let's practice step by step.

Step 1. Parse

In pairs, mark '/' or '//' at proper places. '/' means 'pause', '//' means 'stop'. And read the announcement with proper parses.

FA: Flight Attendant

🔔 FA: Good morning (afternoon, evening),( ) ladies and gentlemen.( ) Captain (Mr. Nicholas) and the entire crew( ) would like to welcome you aboard/ Korea Air,( ) a member of Sky Team.( ) This is flight (701) bound for (Tokyo)/ code-sharing with (Delta Airlines).( )

Our flight time to (Tokyo) today( ) will be (2)hour(s) and (10)minute(s). ( ) During the flight,( ) our cabin crew will be happy to assist you( ) in any way we can.( )

In preparation for departure,( ) please fasten your seatbelt( ) and return your seat and tray table( )to the upright position.( ) You are permitted( ) to use your electronic devices during the flight,( ) as long as they are set to 'Flight Mode'.( )

However,( ) larger devices such as laptop computers( ) must be stowed under your seat( ) or in the overhead bins( ) during take off and landing. ( ) Please ( ) fully cooperate with cabin crew( ) who act as safety officers during the flight.( )

For your safety,( ) please direct your attention( ) to the video screens( )(or cabin crew) for safety information.//

Step 2. Intonation

: In pairs, read the announcement with proper intonation.

√ When you pause (/), your intonation will rise. ↗

√ When you stop(//), your intonation will fall. ↘

Step 3. Pronunciation

: In pairs, read the announcement with clear pronunciation.

√ There are certain pronunciation sounds that you should pay attention to.

√ Discriminating the following sounds are important to deliver clear message.

p/f, b/v, l/r, e.g. **p**assenger/ **f**asten, o**v**erhead **b**in, **l**adies/ **r**eturn

√**'The'** in front of vowels such as **'a, e i, o, u'** will be pronounced as **[ðI]**.

Practice Zone

: Fill in the blanks with your partner to practice out loud.

Welcome Announcement

✈ Practice the following announcement script by producing proper parse, intonation and pronunciation. Be careful of pronunciating words in bold letters.

FA: Flight Attendant

🔔 FA: Good morning, **ladies** and gentlemen.// Captain Mr. Nicholas and **the** entire crew/ would **like** to welcome you aboard/ Korea Air,/ a member of Sky Team.// This is **flight** 701 **bound for** Tokyo,/ code-sharing with Delta Airlines.//

Our flight time to Tokyo today/ will be 2 hours and 10 minutes.// During the flight,/ our cabin crew will be happy to assist you/ in any way we can.//

In preparation for departure,/ please fasten your seatbelt/ and return your seat and tray table /to the upright position.// You are permitted/ to use your electronic devices during the flight,/as long as they are set to 'Flight Mode'.//

However,/ larger devices such as laptop computers/ must be stowed under your seat/ or in the overhead bins/ during take off and landing.// Please fully cooperate with cabin crew/ who act as safety officers during the flight.//

For your safety,/ please direct your attention/ to the video screens/ for safety information.//

Comprehension Zone

: Circle the letter T if the statement is correct, mark a cross at F if the statement is wrong.

1. You can expect to know the flight time, date and the name of a captain after listening to welcome announcement.

   T / F

2. You can't use any electronic devices during take-off and landing in any case.

   T / F

3. Laptop computers should be stowed only in the overhead bin during the flight.

   T / F

4. Flight attendants are safety officers of the cabin.

   T / F

5. When you make an announcement, the intonation rises when you stop at a period mark.

   T / F

Practice Zone

: Fill in the blanks with your partner to practice out loud.

Farewell Announcement

1. In pairs, mark '/' or '//' at proper places. '/' means 'pause', '//' means 'stop'. Read the announcement with proper parses.
2. Practice the following announcement script by producing proper pause, intonation and pronunciation.

FA: Flight Attendant

🔔 FA: **Ladies** and gentlemen,( ) welcome to Seoul Incheon international airport.( )
The **local** time here in Seoul is( ) 7:08 in the morning,( ) on Saturaday, ( ) the 7th of May.( )

[DELAY] We are sorry **for** the delay( ) due to aircraft connection.( ) We appreciate your understanding and **patience**.( )

For your safety,( ) **please** keep your set belt **fastened**( ) until the captain turns off the seat belt sign.( ) **Refrain from** using your mobile **phone** ( ) utill you deplane.( )

When opening **the** overhead **bins**,( ) **please** be careful of contents( ) that may have moved during the **flight**.( ) Also,( ) **please** make sure( ) that there are no items **left** in your seat **pocket** ( ) or under the seat.

On **behalf** of **the** entire crew,( ) we would **like** to express our sincere thanks ( ) to all of you **for flying** Asiana Airlines,( ) a star alliance member. ( ) We hope to see you soon.( )

Comprehension Zone

: Fill in the blanks with appropriate words in the word box.

1. Long flight time without meal needed ____________ to me.
2. I really ____________ flight attendants' sincere care in spite of full flight.
3. Aircraft ____________ is very common reason of delayed departure.
4. Please ____________ your gratitude first before you say 'No' when you are invited to a dinner.
5. I enjoyed the ________ part of the movie.
6. The customs officer examined the ___________ of my bag.
7. Please be careful not to leave your belongings when you ___________.
8. Please __________ from smoking in the cabin.

Word Box

refrain	appreciate	express	connection
entire	contents	deplane	patience

Wrap Up Activity

Tongue Twisters for Fun

① Let the four poor flees flee, please.

② Betty loves the velvet vest best.

③ A loyal warrior will rarely worry why we rule.

④ Lesley loves Roger, but Roger doesn't love Lesley. Roger rather likes Lucy.

⑤ Give papa a cup of proper coffee in a copper coffee cup.

⑥ Frivolous fat fanny fried fresh fish furiously.

⑦ Near an ear, a nearer ear, a nearly eerie ear.

⑧ The big black bug bit the big black bear, but the big black bear bit the big black bug back!

⑨ In Latin, "verb" means 'word', "verbose" means 'using many words', and "verbal" means 'of words'.

⑩ A certain young fellow named Beebee wish to marry a lady named Phoebe, "But", he said. "I must see what the minister's fee be before Phoebe be Phoebe bee Phoebe Beebee".

Exercise

1–5. Please translate the sentences into Korean.

1. This is flight 701 bound for Tokyo, code-sharing with Delta Airlines.

____.

2. During the flight, our cabin crews will be happy to assist you in any way we can.

____.

3. In preparation for departure, please fasten your seatbelt and return your seat and tray table to the upright position.

____.

4. The local time here in Seoul is 10:30 in the morning, on Saturday, the 4th of August.

____.

5. On behalf of the entire crew, we would like to express our sincere thanks to all of you.

____.

Appendix 1

Evaluation Checklist

Self evaluation

☐ Did you speak accurately with target expressions?

☐ Did you speak fluently with proper pause?

☐ Did you pronounce clearly?

☐ Did you use various target vocabulary?

☐ Did you use formal expressions you learned?

☐ Did you speak with well balanced intonation?

☐ Did you control volume effectively?

☐ Did you use proper facial expressions?

☐ Were your posture comfortably upright?

☐ Did you make natural eye contact with the passenger?

Overall comments:

Total score: ______/ 10

Peer evaluation

- ☐ Did your classmate speak accurately with correct forms?
- ☐ Did your classmate speak fluently with proper pause?
- ☐ Did your classmate pronounce clearly?
- ☐ Did your classmate use various vocabulary?
- ☐ Did your classmate use formal expressions you learned?
- ☐ Did your classmate speak with well balanced intonation?
- ☐ Did your classmate control volume effectively?
- ☐ Did your classmate use proper facial expressions?
- ☐ Were your classmate's posture comfortably upright?
- ☐ Did your classmate make natural eye contact with the passenger?

Overall comments:

Total score: ______/ 10

Appendix 2

Service Role Play

 Flight Attendant	Passenger: Angry Seperated from a friend in seating.
 Flight Attendant	Passenger: Angry Delayed boarding in the airport.
 Flight Attendant	Passenger: Angry Meal is not hot enough.
 Flight Attendant	Passenger: Angry Meal choice is not enough.

Flight Attendant

Passenger: Angry
Children are noisy aroud the seat.

Flight Attendant

Passenger: Unsatisfied
Passenger in the next seat is snoring heavily.

Flight Attendant

Passenger: Unsatisfied
Duty-free item has been sold out.

Flight Attendant

Passenger: Nervous
Sweating and shivering before take-off.

Flight Attendant

Passenger: Boring
Asking flight attendant about something to read or eat.

Appendix 3

외국인 고객 호칭 관련

1) 성직자

직급/ 직책	영문 직급/ 직책	호칭의 예
Archbishop	영국 국교회 대주교, 가톨릭 대주교	*Your Excellency* *Archbishop Smith*
Bishop	가톨릭 주교	*Your Excellency* *Bishop Smith*
Brotherhood	수도사	*Brother* *Brother Smith*
Sosterhood	수녀	*Sister* *Sister Mary Angelica*
Cardinal	추기경	*Your Emimmennce* *Cardinal Smith*
Clergyman Protestant	영국 국교회 목사	*Ms./Mr. Smith* *Dr. Smith*
Monsignor Protestant	가톨릭 교회 내 고위성직자	*Monsignor* *Monsignor Smith*
Mother superior	수녀원장	*Reverenend Mother* *Reverendend Mother* *Mary*
Pope	가톨릭 교황	*Your Holiness* *Most Holy Father*

President, Mothermon	몰몬교 수장	*President Smith*
Priest, Catholic	신부	*Father* *Father Smith*
Rabbi	유대교 라비	*Rabbi* *Rabbi Smith* *Dr. Smith*

2) 외국 수반

직급/ 직책	영문 직급/ 직책	호칭의 예
Premier	국무총리	*Mr. /Madam Premier*
Prime Minister	수상	*Mr. /Madam Prime Minister*
President of a Republic	대통령	*Mr. /Madam President*

3) 대사 · 영사

직급/ 직책	영문 직급/ 직책	호칭의 예
Consul, General	총영사	*Mr. /Ms. Smith*
Ambassador, USA	대사	*Mr. / Madam Ambassador*
Ambassador, Foreign	대사	*Excellency,* *Mr. /Madam Ambassador*
Minister	공사	*Mr. /Madam Minister*
Charge d'affaires	대리 공사, 공사 대리	*Mr. /Ms. Smith*

4) 정부 요인

직급/ 직책	영문 직급/ 직책	호칭의 예
Cabinet Members or Secretary/ General of USA	장관	*Mr. /Madam Secretary*
President	대통령	*Mr./ Madam President*
Former President	前 대통령	*Mr./ Madam Smith*
Vice President	부통령	*Mr./ Madam Vice President*
Representative	하원의원	*Mr./ Ms. Smith*
Senator	상원의원	*Senator Smith*
Speaker of the House	하원의장	*Mr./ Madam Speaker*
Mayor	시장	*Mayor Smith* *Mr. Mayor* *Your honor*
Governor	주지사	*Governor* *Governor Smith*

5) 대학 교수

직급/ 직책	영문 직급/ 직책	호칭의 예
Chancellor	영국식 대학총장	*Dr. Smith* *Chancellor Smith*
Dean	대학 학부장	*Dr. Smith* *Dean Smith*
President	미국식 대학총장	*Dr. Smith* *President Smith*
President, Priest	총장(신부)	*Father Smith*
Professor (Assistant)	조교수	*Dr. Smith* *Professor Smith* *Mr./ Ms. Smith*
Professor (full)	전임교수	*Dr. Smith* *Professor Smith*

6) 군인

직급/ 직책	영문 직급/ 직책	호칭의 예
Admiral	해군장성/ 제독	*Admiral Smith*
Captain	함장/ 해군대령	*Captain Smith*
General	육군대장, 장군	*General Smith*
Commander	해군중령/ 군대 사령관	*Commander Smith*
Major	육군소령, 공군소령	*Major Smith*
Sergeant	하사/중사/상사	*Sergeant Smith*
Sergeant Major	주임상사	*Sergeant Major Smith*
Lieutenant	육군중위/ 상관대리	*Lieutenant Smith*

7) 경제인

직급/ 직책	영문 직급/ 직책	호칭의 예
Chairman, President	회장	*Chairman Smith* *President Smith*
CEO (Chief Executive Officer)	최고경영자, 대표이사	*CEO Smith*

Summary of the Units

Unit 1

Expressions

1. May I help you?: 무엇을 도와드릴까요?
2. I'd like to reserve a ticket to NewYork.: 뉴욕행 항공권을 예약하고 싶습니다.
3. Which class would you like, sir?: 어떤 등급의 좌석을 원하십니까?
4. How many are there in your party?: 일행이 몇 분이십니까?
5. You're booked on Asiana Airlines flight 222 to New York on May 8.: 5월 8일 아시아나 항공 뉴욕행 항공권이 예약되었습니다.

Unit 2

Expressions

1. May I see your ticket and passport?: 항공권과 여권을 보여주시겠습니까?
2. Would you like an aisle seat or a window seat?: 통로 좌석을 원하십니까, 창가 좌석을 원하십니까?
3. How many baggages would you like to check?: 몇 개의 짐을 부치시겠습니까?
4. We'll let you know as soon as possible.: 최대한 빠르게 알려드리도록 하겠습니다.

Unit 3

Expressions

1. Let me report on emergency and security equipments.: 비상 및 보안 장비에 대해 보고드리겠습니다.
2. I'd like to report on the meals and service items.: 식사와 서비스 물품에 대해 보고드리겠습니다.
3. It must have been used before.: 전에 사용되었던 것이 분명합니다.
4. All safety and security items are okay including smoke detector in lavatory.: 화장실 연기감지장치를 포함한 모든 안전 및 보안 장비 이상 없습니다.

Unit 4

Expressions

1. Welcome aboard.: 탑승을 환영합니다.
2. May I see your boarding pass, please?: 탑승권을 보여주시겠습니까?
3. Please take this aisle.: 이쪽 통로를 이용하시겠습니까?
4. It's in the back/front/middle/the other side of the cabin.: 기내 뒷쪽/앞쪽/가운데쪽/건너편쪽입니다.
5. You're welcome.: 천만에요.
6. Enjoy your flight, sir/ma'am.: 즐거운 비행 되십시오.
7. Your seat number is 45K.: 손님 좌석은 45K입니다.
8. Please come this way.: 이쪽으로 오십시오.
9. It's a window/an aisle seat.: 창가/통로쪽 자리입니다.

Unit 5

Expressions

1. May I have a glass of water?: 물 한잔 주시겠습니까?
2. Let me get it for you, right away.: 금방 가져다 드리겠습니다.
3. Let me check if there's what I can do.: 제가 도와드릴 수 있는지 알아보겠습니다.
4. Thank you for waiting.: 기다려 주셔서 감사합니다.
5. Please come with me.: 저를 따라 와주십시오.
6. Thank you for your cooperation: 협조해 주셔서 감사합니다.
7. There has been a mistake in seat arrangement.: 좌석 배정에 문제가 있었나

봅니다.

8. I'm terribly sorry for the inconvenience.: 불편을 드려 대단히 죄송합니다.
9. If you need anything during the flight, please let us know.: 비행중 필요한 것이 있으시면 알려주십시오.

Unit 6

Expressions

1. Is this bag yours?: 이 가방은 당신 것입니까?
2. I'm afraid all the aisles should be cleaned during take off and landing.: 이착륙 동안에는 모든 기내 통로가 치워져 있어야 합니다.
3. Please put your bag in the overhead bin.: 가방은 머리위 보관함에 넣어 주십시오.
4. This bag is too heavy to keep in the overhead bin.: 이 가방은 너무 커서 머리위 보관함에 보관할 수 없습니다.
5. Would you keep your bag under the seat in front of you?: 손님의 가방은 앞좌석 아래에 보관해 주시겠습니까?
6. May I keep it in the closet?: 그 짐을 옷장에 보관해 드려도 되겠습니까?
7. Please wait in your seat.: 좌석에서 기다려 주십시오.

Unit 7

Expressions

1. This is an emergency exit door for emergency.: 이 좌석은 비상시만을 위한 비상구입니다.
2. Passengers in emergency exit seats are supposed to help flight atendants to evacuate passengers in emergency.: 비상구 좌석에 앉아계신 승객들께서는 비상시 승무원을 도와 승객들의 탈출을 도우셔야 합니다.
3. We are preparing for take-off.: 이륙준비를 하고 있습니다.
4. Please fasten your seatbelt.: 좌석벨트를 매주시기 바랍니다.
5. Return your seat back to the upright position, please.: 좌석 등받이를 제자리로 해 주 시기 바랍니다.
6. We are expecting some turbulence.: 불안정한 기류관계로 기체가 약간 흔들릴 것으로 예상됩니다.
7. Please also check if the seat belt of your child is securely fastened.: 자녀의 좌석 벨트가 잘 매어져 있는지 또한 확인해 주십시오.

Unit 8

Expressions

1. Would you care for some drinks before your meal?: 식사 전 음료 하시겠습니까?
2. We have red wine and white wine from California or Bordeaux.: 캘리포니아산, 혹은 보르도산 레드와인과 화이트 와인이 준비되어 있습니다.
3. Which one would you prefer?: 어느 것으로 하시겠습니까?

4. Excuse me, we are serving dinner.: 실례지만, 저녁 식사서비스 중입니다.
5. We have a choice of beef steak or chicken with rice.: 쇠고기 스테이크와 닭고기 덮밥이 준비되어 있습니다.
6. I'm sorry, sir. Bibimbap is not available in this flight.: 죄송하지만, 이 구간에서는 비빔밥이 서비스 되지 않습니다.
7. Instead, we have chicken with rice.: 그 대신에 닭고기 덮밥이 준비되어 있습니다.
8. Would you care for a drink with your meal?: 식사와 함께 음료하시겠습니까?
9. Do you need anything else? 그 밖에 필요한 것이 있으십니까?
10. Would you care for coffee?: 커피하시겠습니까?
11. Another flight attendant will serve tea very soon.: 다른 승무원이 곧 차를 서비스하겠습니다.
12. May I have your cup here on the tray?: 이 쟁반에 컵을 올려 주시겠습니까?
13. It might be hot, please be careful.: 뜨거울 수 있으니 조심해 주십시오.

Unit 9

Expressions

1. Would you like to purchase duty-free items?: 면세품 주문하시겠습니까?
2. We have liquors, perfumes, cosmetics, chocolates and gift items.: 면세품으로는 술, 향수, 화장품, 초콜릿 그리고 선물용 제품들이 있습니다.
3. How would you like to pay, by credit or cash?: 지불화폐는 카드로 하시겠습니까? 아니면 현금으로 하시겠습니까?

4. Here's your perfume and the receipt. Please double check your order.: 여기 향수와 영수증입니다. 주문을 다시 한번 확인해 주십시오.
5. May I take your order, sir?: 주문하시겠습니까?
6. I'm terribly sorry, sir. It has been sold out.: 대단히 죄송하지만, 그 제품은 품절되었습니다.

Unit 10

Expressions

1. Let me go and check as soon as possible.: 제가 가서 최대한 빠르게 확인해보겠습니다.
2. I'm really sorry, sir. Your vegetarian meal is not on board.: 손님, 대단히 죄송합니다만, 채식 식사가 탑재되지 않았습니다.
3. There may have been a mistake in reservation.: 예약과정에 문제가 있었던 것 같습니다.
4. Please accept our apology.: 저희의 사과를 받아주십시오.
5. We appreciate your understanding.: 양해해 주셔서 감사합니다.
6. While you're waiting, would you like some hot drinks?: 기다리시는동안 뜨거운 음료 하시겠습니까?
7. I hope you'll get well soon.: 금방 회복되시길 바랍니다.

Unit 11

Expressions

1. Did you order a wheelchair at the arrival airport?: 도착 공항에 휠체어를 주문하셨습니까?
2. Would you like to deplane first or later?: 먼저 내리시겠습니까, 나중에 내리시겠습니까?
3. Did you have a good rest?: 편히 쉬셨습니까?
4. Let me guide you to one of our ground staffs waiting at the arrival airport.: 제가 도착 공항에서 기다리고 있는 저희 직원중 한 명에게 모셔다 드리겠습니다.
5. We are landing shortly.: 곧 착륙하겠습니다.
6. Estimated arrival time is 11:05 am. in local time.: 도착 예정 시간은 현지 시간으로 오전 11시 5분 입니다.

Unit 12

Expressions

1. Please have your passport and other entry documents ready.: 여권과 다른 입국서류를 준비해 주십시오.
2. All foreigners entering into Korea, must fill out the arrival card.: 한국에 입국하시는 모든 외국인 손님께서는 입국신고서를 작성하셔야 합니다.
3. Do you want me to help you with the arrival card?: 입국 신고서 작성에 도움이 필요하십니까?
4. All apssengers must fill out the customs declaration form.: 모든 손님께서

는 세관신고서를 작성하셔야 합니다.

5. Only one form is needed for family members traveling together.: 가족당 한 매만 작성하시면 됩니다.
6. Here's a customs form that is written in English. 여기 영어로 된 세관신고서를 드리겠습니다.

Unit 13

Tips for Inflight Announcement

✈ How to make a good in-flight announcement.

When you make an announcement, you have to focus on delivering the flight information clearly such as the flight number, flight time, destination, sir name of captain, and where the passengers can stow their belongings. Moreover, welcoming and caring atmosphere should also be made carefully. To make a clear announcement, parsing, intonation, pronunciation is the key features.

〈Step 1. Parse〉

In pairs, mark '/' or '//' at proper places. '/' means **'pause'**, '//' means **'stop'**. Read the announcement with proper parses.

〈Step2. Intonation〉

: In pairs, read the announcement with proper intonation.

√ When you pause (/), your intonation will rise. ↗

√ When you stop (//), your intonation will fall. ↘

〈Step 3. Pronunciation〉

: In pairs, read the announcement with clear pronunciation.

√There are certain pronunciation sounds that you should pay attention to.

√Discriminating the following sounds are important to deliver clear message.

p/f, b/v, l/r,

e.g. **p**assenger/ **f**asten, o**v**erhead **b**in, **l**adies/ **r**eturn

√'The' in front of vowels such as **'a, e i, o, u'** will be pronounced as **[ðI]**.

References

Anderson. N. J. and Nunan D. (2008). *Practical English Language Teaching: Reading.* McGraw-Hill ELT.

Avery P., and Ehrlich. S. (2008). *Teaching American English Pronunciation.* Oxford University Press.

Bailey K. M., and Nunan. D. (2005). *Practical English Language Teaching: Speaking.* McGraw-Hill ELT.

Brown. H. D., and Abeywickrama. P. (2010). *Language Assesment.* Pearson Longman.

Cordell. J. (2007). *Cambridge Business English Activities*. Cambridge University Press.

De Botton. A. (2010). *A Week at the Airport.* Profilebooks.

Dudly-Evans. T., and St John, M. -J. (2011). *Developments in English for Specific Purposes.* Cambridge University Press.

Harmer. J. (2013). *How to Teach Writing*. Pearson.

Harmer. J. (2011). *The Practice of English Language Teaching.* Pearson Longman.

Helgesen. M., and Brown. S. (2012). *Practical English Language Teaching: Listening.* McGraw-Hill ELT.

HyunOk. L. (2018). *All about English Interview for Cabin Crew* (pp. 53-57). Ewha Womans University.

Larsen-Freeman. D., and Anderson. M. (2015). *Techniques & Principles in Language Teaching.* Oxford University Press.

NCS. (2017). *National Competency Standards.* Human Resources Development Service of Korea:

https://www.ncs.go.kr/unity/hth01/hth0101/selectNcsModuleReport.do

Nunan D., and Bailey. K. M. (2009). *Exploring Second Language Classroom Research.* Heinle Cengage Learning.

Richards. J. C. (2014). *Second Language Writing*. Cambridge Language Writing.

Answer Key

Unit 1

Practice Zone: Reservation

May, reserve, many, booked

Practice Zone: Ticketing

May I, reservation, May I, How, signature

Reading Comprehension

Q1. symbolized (상징했다) 혹은 meant (의미했다)
Q2. robot

Unit 2

Practice Zone: Check-in

an, aisle, How, many, scale, baggage, claim,

Practice Zone: Baggage Claim

May, I, claim, describe, possible

Reading Comprehension

Q1. the Warsaw convention
Q2. Montreal Protocol
Q3. $100(₩120,000)

Unit 3

Practice Zone: Pre-flight Check 1

report, have, been, smoke, detecter, report, fixed

Practice Zone: Pre-flight Check 2

turns, well, seem, check

Reading Comprehension

Q1. prohibited, restrictions

Q2. To protect passengers or crews from being bitten or contaminated.

Q3. Describe your experiences

Example: *I've met a dog at a shopping mall last week. It suddenly jumped out of the elevater when I was waiting. It was quite big so everyone seemed to be annoyed and frightened including me and I felt even embarrassed when the owner did not try to control it. I understand the emotional support anmal is like a familiy member for them though they should also understand the ettiqutte in public places.*

Unit 4

Practice Zone: At Boarding Zone

aboard, May, I, take, welcome, enjoy

Practice Zone: At Duty Zone

Welcome, help, pass, come, right, welcome, enjoy

Reading Comprehension

Q1. relationship (관계)

Q2. eye contact

Q3. Describe your experiences

Example: *When I worked at a restaurant, I welcomed customers by saying 'Good morning' with bright smile and then asked if they had a reseravation. I also asked how many there were in their groups. Then I guided them to a proper seat.*

Unit 5

Practice Zone: Passenger Request- Drink

May, I, Let me

Practice Zone: Passenger Request- Seperated Seats

Let, me, check, Thank, you, for, come

Practice Zone: Double Seat

Excuse, boarding, pass, bother, cooperation, seat, arrangement,
May, I, terribly, sorry, know

Reading Comprehension

Q1. Because most passengers expect the cabin crew to know a lot more than we think, and ask various questons to the crew member.

Q2. gravity

Q3. An aircraft will not be able to fly.

Unit 6

Practice Zone: Baggage in the Aisle

yours, afraid, during,
put, pleasure

Practice Zone: Heavy Baggage

too, to, seat, flight

Practice Zone: Oversize Baggage

overhead, bin, seat, landing, wait

Reading Comprehension

Q1. A good service can be achieved by collaborating of all crew members.

Q2. Achieving an efficient service design, Determining the overall image of the airline.

Unit 7

Practice Zone: Passengers in Emergency Exit Seats

emergency, help, evacuate, cooperation

Practice Zone: Safety Check before Take-off

preparing, fasten, return, button

Practice Zone: Expecting Turbulence

turbulence, seat, belt, back, fastened, return

Reading Comprehension

Q1. Beijing, China

Q2. wore prosthetic leg

Q3. The reasons were because he had been using it since he was young and he had no problem with helping passengers in emergency. And he had been used emergency exit seat for several times till then.

Unit 8

Practice Zone: Aperitif- Beverage before Meal Service

meal, have, Which, Certainly

Practice Zone: Meal Service

serving, choice, not, available, Instead, care, for, else

Practice Zone: Coffee or Tea Service

care, for, Another, here, be, careful

Reading Comprehension

Q1. Burkina Faso
Q2. African with French citizenship
Q3. Turkish nationality

Unit 9

Practice Zone: Duty Free Sales 1

duty, free, duty, free, have, like
pay, credit, soon, waiting, double

Practice Zone: Duty Free Sales 2

order, sold, out, care, moment

Reading Comprehension

Q1. 1 litre
Q2. United States of America
Q3. Singapore

Unit 10

Practice Zone: Complaints- Meal Service

name, as, soon, as, on, board, list
mistake, apology, waiting, available, try, appreciate

Practice Zone: Complaints- Cabin Condition
get, temperature, While, Certainly
get, well, help

Reading Comprehension
Q1. Apologize sincerely.
Q2. ②

Unit 11

Practice Zone: Special Passenger Care- Wheelchair
arrival, deplane, Certainly

Practice Zone: Special Passenger Care- UM
have, land, ground, staffs, recognize

Practice Zone: Collection of Service Items
shortly, time, Estimated, seat, back, stay

Unit 12

Practice Zone: Arrival Card
foreigners, with, know

Practice Zone: Customs Declaration Form
declaration, one, is, written, know

Practice Zone: Documentation Announcement
documents, except, customs, one, two,

Reading Comprehension
Q1. Because vague answers or words will prolong the interview process.
Q2. ⓑ, ⓒ, ⓔ
Q3. eye contact, vague answers or words, only when you understand the question

Unit 13

Comprehension Zone

1. F (date is normally shown in farewell announcement)
2. F
3. F
4. T
5. F

Comprehension Zone

1. patience
2. appreciate
3. connection
4. express
5. entire
6. contents
7. deplane
8. refrain

저 | 자 | 소 | 개

■ **이현옥**

이화여자대학교 테솔/영어교육학석사

전. 이화여자대학교 테솔/영어교육학강사
수원과학대학교 외래교수
아시아나항공 국제선 부사무장

현. H Communication 대표이사
국제대학교 항공서비스학과 겸임교수

■ **임영수**

경기대학교 일반대학원 관광학박사

현. 국제대학교 국제교류센터장
국제대학교 항공서비스학과장
E&P consulting (주) 대표이사
코레일 경영자문 등 다수 공기관 자문위원

항공서비스 영어
Basic Airline Service English

1판 1쇄 인쇄 — 2019년 7월 15일
1판 1쇄 발행 — 2019년 7월 19일

저 자 - 이현옥 임영수

발 행 인 - 강철원
발 행 처 - 양성원
주 소 - 경기도 파주시 검산로 173번길 29-20
전 화 - 031-946-3861(代)
팩 스 - 031-946-3864
이 메 일 - tnwpub@naver.com
홈페이지 - tnwpub.co.kr
출판등록 - 2015년 8월 31일 제 2015-000211 호

ISBN 979-11-6126-187-4

정가 18,000원

※ 저자와 협의하여 인지는 생략합니다.
※ 저작권법 제136조(권리의 침해죄)에 따라 위반자는 5년 이하의 징역 또는 5천만 원 이하의 벌금에 처하거나 이를 병과할 수 있습니다.